Churchill

THE WICKED WIT OF
WINSTON CHURCHILL

THE
WICKED WIT
OF
WINSTON
CHURCHILL

Compiled, edited and introduced by
Dominique Enright

MICHAEL O'MARA BOOKS LIMITED

First published in Great Britain in 2001 by
Michael O'Mara Books Limited
9 Lion Yard, Tremadoc Road
London SW4 7NQ

A CIP catalogue record for this book
is available from the British Library

ISBN 1-85479-529-5

5 7 9 10 8 6

Designed and typeset by Martin Bristow

Printed and bound in Finland
by WS Bookwell, Juva

Contents

'It is a good thing for an uneducated man to read books of quotations.' These words, from *My Early Life*, 1930, are not as arrogant as they might sound. Churchill, who never claimed to be an educated man, goes on to describe how he read *Bartlett's Familiar Quotations* 'intently', adding that 'the quotations when engraved upon the memory give you good thoughts' and lead you to read the authors' works.

Elsewhere he advises: 'Verify your quotations': not always the easiest thing to do with Churchill, whose memory was crowded with phrases remembered, coined, embellished, used more than once, but not necessarily word for word.

Introduction

Sir Winston Leonard Spencer Churchill
was born in 1874 at Blenheim Palace, Oxford-
shire, the eldest son of Lord Randolph Churchill
and his American wife, and a nephew of the Duke
of Marlborough. Despite an undistinguished career
at Harrow, he attended the RMA, Sandhurst, before
being gazetted to the 4th Hussars. Following service
in India and on the North-West Frontier, he took
part in the Nile Expeditionary Force in the Sudan
in 1898, and was attached to the 21st Lancers when
that regiment made its famous mounted charge
against the dervishes during the Battle of Omdur-
man. As a newspaper correspondent during the
Boer War of 1899–1901 he was captured when the
armoured train he was travelling in was ambushed
and derailed, but later successfully escaped his cap-
tors and made an epic journey back to British lines.
He was present at a number of the most famous
battles of the campaign, including Spion Kop.

Churchill entered Parliament as a Conservative
MP in 1900 but, finding himself increasingly at odds
with the party, in 1904 crossed the floor of the House
and joined the Liberal Party, becoming Under-Secretary for the Colonies in 1906 and President of the
Board of Trade two years later, in which post he
introduced labour exchanges. Appointed Home Secretary in 1910, he was involved in the Siege of Sidney
Street the following year, and not long afterwards

changed his post for that of First Lord of the Admiralty, and thereafter worked furiously to prepare the Royal Navy for the war with Germany that he knew must come; he also worked tirelessly on the development and deployment of tanks, an invention for which (as was later officially acknowledged) he was partly responsible. In 1915 he resigned in the face of blame for the costly failure of the Dardanelles and Gallipoli operations, and went to France to take command of an infantry battalion on the Western Front. He returned to Britain in 1916 and in 1917 took up the post of Minister of Munitions in the Coalition government now headed by Lloyd George. He was Secretary for War and Air from 1919–21, but in 1924 changed allegiance once more when he was elected to a different constituency as a 'constitutionalist' Conservative; from then until 1929 he served as Chancellor of the Exchequer.

Without office in the 1930s under Ramsay MacDonald's National government and the succeeding Tory administrations, he increasingly warned from the backbenches of the dangers of German rearmament, of appeasement of the dictators, and of Britain's absolute lack of preparedness for war, referring to the Munich settlement of 1938 as 'a total and unmitigated defeat'. The fall of Norway in May 1940, and the imminent threat to British forces in France and to Britain herself, led to a vote of no confidence in the administration headed by Neville Chamberlain, whom Churchill succeeded as Prime Minister, immediately forming a Coalition government. Despite the disasters in Belgium and France, victory in the Battle of Britain, followed by successes at sea and in North Africa, helped to stiffen the country's sinews, aided immeasurably by Churchill's leadership and his oratory. His close personal friendship with President Roosevelt ensured American support and, following Japanese and German declarations of war against the USA in December 1941, did much to smooth the often rocky path of inter-Allied co-operation, while his ability both to flatter and to stand up to Stalin promoted a relationship with the Soviet Union that helped to ensure the defeat of the Axis. After German defeats in North Africa and Russia, and American naval victories over the Japanese in the Pacific, the tide of war began to turn, and Churchill increasingly directed his formidable talents to the total defeat of Germany, Italy and Japan and the maintenance of the Triple Alliance which was to bring that about. He was not to share in the final triumph, however; in the general election of July 1945, two months after Germany's unconditional surrender, the war-weary British people voted the Labour Party into power, and Churchill handed over the premiership to Clement Attlee.

He remained an untiring leader of the Opposition, while his fame and reputation ensured that he maintained an overwhelming presence on the international stage. In 1951, aged seventy-seven, he became Prime Minister again, resigning in 1955 in favour of the much younger Anthony Eden, although he stayed on as a backbencher well into his old age, until failing health forced him to give up his seat in Parliament. He died, full of years and honours, in 1965 and, after a magnificent state funeral, was buried in the graveyard of the tiny parish church close to Blenheim Palace, the house in which he had been born.

*

'The characteristic of a great man is his power to leave a lasting impression on people he meets,' Churchill once said. Was he thinking of himself? He was certainly not blind to his own stature. He was one of the few people who can truly be said to have been larger than life. His life was not only long but it was full and varied – full of friends, and of enemies; full of action and creativity, of argument and ruthlessness. There were many who loved him, many who hated him, and many, it seems, who both loved and hated him. Exuberant and spoiled, childish and childlike, kind and cruel, enquiring but pig-headed, hardworking and generous but conceited and determined to be centre-stage . . . Churchill was all of these things. Remembered as a political leader, as a wartime strategist, and as the last of the great public orators, Churchill's fame also rests upon his many books, notably his histories. These include *The World Crisis* (four volumes, 1923–9), *Marlborough* (four volumes, 1933–8), *The Second World War* (six volumes,

1948–54) and *A History of the English-Speaking Peoples* (four volumes, 1956–8), besides numerous volumes of speeches and broadcasts, volumes of autobiography, a biography of his father, one rather poor novel, *Savrola* ('I have consistently urged my friends to abstain from reading it.'), and countless articles, including some on painting which were published as a book, *Painting as a Pastime*. Altogether he published more words than Charles Dickens and Walter Scott together – 'more books than Moses,' he once joked.

He painted well enough for the painter Sir John Lavery to say: 'Had he chosen painting instead of statesmanship I believe he would have been a great master with the brush', and his work, under the name Charles Morin, was accepted by the Louvre. He had the inventive imagination and mental application to devise the tank: '. . . fit up a number of steam tractors with small armoured shelters, in which men and machine-guns could be placed, which would be bullet-proof . . . The caterpillar system would enable trenches to be crossed quite easily, and the weight of the machine would destroy all wire entanglements,' he wrote to the Prime Minister, Herbert Asquith, in January 1915. In addition, he played polo, was a fine shot – and enjoyed brick-laying, even accepting an invitation to join the Amalgamated Union of Building Trade Workers. For someone whose formal education was less than full, this list of achievements is especially impressive. However it may be, Churchill himself suggested that his slow progress at school might have been a hidden blessing: 'By being so long in the lowest form I gained an immense advantage over the cleverer boys . . . I got into my bones the essential structure of the normal British sentence – which is a noble thing.'

'He mobilized the English language and sent it into battle,' said John F. Kennedy in 1963 when granting Churchill US citizenship. There are those who believe that during the Second World War it was the inspiring power of his speeches that kept up morale and ultimately led the Allies to victory. Others were less enchanted: 'In private conversation,' complained the writer and administrator Lionel Curtis, 'he tries on speeches like a man trying on ties in his bedroom to see how he would look in them.'

Of the orator and his audience, Churchill said:

Before he can inspire them with any emotion, he must be swayed by it himself. When he would rouse their indignation, his heart is filled with anger. Before he can move their tears, his own must flow. To convince them, he must himself believe. His opinions may change as their impressions fade, but every orator means what he says at the moment he says it. He is never consciously insincere.

Asked by Adlai Stevenson, in 1955, on what he based his oratorical style, Churchill told him: 'America – and Bourke Cockran, who taught me to use every note of the human voice as if playing an organ.' Churchill had met Cockran, a New York politician, on his first visit to the United States sixty years before, and they remained friends over the years. Cockran, said Churchill, 'could play on every emotion and hold thousands of people riveted . . . when he spoke.' Yet it is Churchill who is remembered for his oratory. It might be because Churchill was a very emotional man himself – and not ashamed of showing his feelings ('I blub an awful lot, you know. You'll have to get used to it,' he warned Anthony Montague Browne soon after the latter's appointment as his Private Secretary) – that he could strike a chord in the emotions of his listeners. Which is not to say that he did not also manipulate his words: 'There is no finer investment for any community than putting milk into babies,' he said in a 1943 radio broadcast – he had a fine ear for the heartstring-tugging phrase and the chorus of 'Aahs' can almost be heard. This was also, however, an aspect of his soft-heartedness – which could on occasion descend to the absurd, as when this ruthless politician – who had called upon the nation to fight, fight, fight, and never surrender – while watching a film of *Oliver Twist* at home put a hand over his dog Rufus's eyes so that Rufus would not see Bill Sikes drown his dog. Or as when he would hand a book to his secretary saying to 'put it away, Toby has read it' – Toby being his budgerigar who, along with a cat, had the run of his bedroom (and of his guests – Jock Colville, one of Churchill's Private Secretaries, relates counting fourteen budgie droppings on Rab Butler's bald head one day when, as Chancellor of the Exchequer, Butler had spent some time at Churchill's bedside going through budget papers with the Prime Minister, who liked to work in bed. Butler himself told of an earlier such visit to Chequers, in 1943 – he had found the Prime Minister in bed, with Nelson the cat curled up on his feet: 'This cat,' declared Churchill, ' does more for the war effort than you do. He acts as a hot-water bottle and saves fuel and power.')

Churchill's ability with words was not only employed in sonorous speeches (most of which were fine oratory but not wicked wit), but also in his impish – indeed, often childish – sense of humour. He could not resist making a quip – occasionally even when he did not actually mean what he was saying – to the extent that over the years many witty remarks whose provenance is in fact far from certain have been ascribed to him. Some he denied – but might well have been responsible for; others that he was not responsible for he might well have been quite happy to have credited to him. Thus of those witticisms and stories that follow not every single one can be guaranteed to have originated with Churchill – but they could have, and some he would have liked to have coined. Whistler's comment to Oscar Wilde when the playwright remarked, 'How I wish I had said that' comes to mind: 'You will, Oscar, you will.'

DOMINIQUE ENRIGHT
July 2001

The political arena is famously a battleground where the weapons are words, and many are the insults that flow back and forth across the parliamentary floor.

✳

'The world today is ruled by harassed politicians absorbed in getting into office or turning out the other man so that not much room is left for debating great issues on their merits.'

✳

'Politics are almost as exciting as war, and quite as dangerous. In war you can only be killed once, but in politics many times,' Churchill is said to have remarked in 1920 – he had many more political deaths to live through. On one occasion, in 1916, when he was in bad odour with the Conservatives he wrote to the Prime Minister Lloyd George, who was planning a trip to Russia, 'Don't get torpedoed; for if I am left alone your colleagues will eat me.'

✳

Asked what qualities a politician required, Churchill replied, 'The ability to foretell what is going to happen tomorrow, next week, next month, and next year. And to have the ability afterwards to explain why it didn't happen.'

At a press conference in Cairo in 1943, however, he admitted: 'I always avoid prophesying beforehand, because it is much better policy to prophesy after the event has already taken place.' (In 1927, he had remarked to the House, 'A hopeful disposition is not the sole qualification to be a prophet.')

✳

When Churchill was still a Liberal and serving under Herbert Asquith, the Liberal Prime Minister, a Conservative MP in conversation with Churchill described Asquith as 'wicked'. Churchill thought of Asquith, and then of Arthur Balfour, the Conservative leader of the Opposition: 'No,' he said, 'Balfour is wicked and moral. Asquith is good and immoral.'

✳

'When I was called upon to be Prime Minister, now nearly two years ago, there were not many applicants for the job. Since then perhaps the market has improved,' Churchill informed the House of Commons in January 1942. The likelihood is that the market had not yet improved – and would not until after the end of the war. It was clearly not the world's greatest job during the war years as a contemporary handwritten note from Churchill to Stanley Baldwin, a former Conservative Prime Minister, attests: 'I cannot say that I am enjoying being Prime Minister very much.'

'No one pretends that democracy is perfect or all-wise. Indeed, it has been said that democracy is the worst form of Government except all those other forms that have been tried from time to time.' Churchill uttered these words in a speech to the House of Commons in November 1947 – he had by then seen some of those 'other forms' of government and had not liked them.

✳

To an MP bouncing up and down with interruption after interruption during one of his speeches, an exasperated Churchill advised, 'The honourable gentleman should really not generate more indignation than he can conveniently contain.'

✳

'The high belief in the perfection of man is appropriate in a man of the cloth but not in a prime minister.'

✳

When passed a very long and turgidly written memorandum on some worthy but uninspiring subject, the elderly Prime Minister weighed the thick wad of paper in his hands and commented, 'This paper by its very length defends itself against the risk of being read.'

Churchill's definition of a parliamentary candidate was succinct: 'He is asked to stand, he wants to sit, he is expected to lie.'

✳

Describing the difference between a candidate and an MP: 'One stands for a place – the other sits for it.'

✳

'The Conservative Party is not a party but a conspiracy.' (These words were uttered during Churchill's spell as a Liberal.)

And not much later, he was heard to remark 'Tory democracy is a democracy which supports the Tories,' and also: 'The Tory fault – a yearning for mediocrity.' Some years later, in 1923, he announced 'I am what I have always been – a Tory Democrat. Force of circumstances has compelled me to serve with another party . . .'

✳

'Reconstructing a Cabinet is like solving a kaleidoscopic jigsaw puzzle.'

✳

'Headmasters have powers at their disposal with which Prime Ministers have never been invested.'

Even in the House of Commons, Churchill could be pretty childish – deliberately so, probably to keep the attention of his listeners. Thus exchanges such as this one, in April 1941:

WSC: 'We have all heard of how Dr Guillotine was executed by the instrument he invented – '
Sir Herbert Samuel: 'He was not.'
WSC: 'Well, he ought to have been.'

✳

During Churchill's 'wilderness years' in the 1930s a number of Baldwin's ministers were being mentioned as candidates for peerages. A couple of them had been particularly hostile to WSC, and, it is said, when a colleague remarked to him that their names were among those being bandied about, and asked him what he thought, his answer was brief and to the point: 'Peerages, no – disappearages, yes.'

✳

'It would be a great reform in politics if wisdom could be made to spread as easily and as rapidly as folly.'

✳

'They are not fit to manage a whelk stall,' Churchill said of the Labour Party in 1945 when he was ousted from the premiership in Labour's favour.

A Member of Parliament's rambling monologue against Churchill's wartime policies was interrupted by the Prime Minister: 'I must warn him that he runs a very grave risk of falling into senility before he is overtaken by age.'

✳

'I do not challenge the honourable gentleman when the truth leaks out of him from time to time.' One of Churchill's political rivals had just interrupted him with a rebutting fact.

✳

While campaigning in 1900, it is said that the young Churchill was doing a spot of canvassing when one of those he approached exclaimed: 'Vote for you? Why, I'd rather vote for the Devil!' 'I understand,' Churchill answered. 'But in case your friend is not running, may I count on your support?'

✳

Not long before Churchill crossed the floor to join the Liberal Party, he remarked of his (then) fellow Conservatives: 'They are a class of right honourable gentlemen – all good men, all honest men – who are ready to make great sacrifices for their opinions, but they have no opinions. They are ready to die for the truth, if only they knew what the truth was.'

'They say you can rat, but you can't re-rat,' Churchill remarked in 1941, referring to changing political parties. He, of course, had re-ratted. He is also said to have observed: 'Anyone can rat, but it takes a certain amount of ingenuity to re-rat.'

'A change of party is usually considered a much more serious breach of consistency than a change of view': ratting clearly needed some justification – 'Some men change their party for the sake of their principles; others change their principles for the sake of their party.' (WSC was very probably familiar with the words attributed to Disraeli: 'Damn your principles! Stick to your party!')

Still on the subject of ratting, in 1920, a fellow Liberal MP crossed the floor to join the ailing Socialist Party, at which Churchill remarked, 'It is the only time I've ever seen a rat swimming towards a sinking ship.'

While, in an exchange in the Commons in 1926 when Churchill was Chancellor of the Exchequer, his Labour predecessor Philip Snowden accused him of switching positions on his budget. Churchill pointed out that there was nothing wrong with change if it was in the right direction, to which Snowden countered that 'The honourable gentleman is an authority on that.'

Churchill retorted happily: 'To improve is to change; to be perfect is to change often.'

'If I valued the honourable gentleman's opinion I might get angry,' WSC responded calmly when an Ulster Member shouted 'Contemptible' during an Irish Home Rule debate in the House.

✳

'I see it is said that leaders should keep their ears to the ground. All I can say is that the British nation will find it very hard to look up to the leaders who are detected in that somewhat ungainly posture.'

✳

'When I am abroad, I always make it a rule never to criticize or attack the government of my own country. I make up for lost time when I get home.' (It was 1947, the government no longer Churchill's.)

✳

'There is not one single social or economic principle or concept in the philosophy of the Russian Bolshevik which has not been realized, carried into action, and enshrined in immutable laws a million years ago by the white ant.'

'The inherent vice of capitalism is the unequal sharing of blessings; the inherent virtue of socialism is the equal sharing of miseries.'

❋

'Trying to maintain good relations with a Communist is like wooing a crocodile. You do not know whether to tickle it under the chin or beat it over the head. When it opens its mouth, you cannot tell whether it is trying to smile or preparing to eat you up.'

❋

Asked in 1952 by a Labour MP if he, the Prime Minister, was aware of the deep concern felt by the British over the question of the Korean conflict, WSC answered, 'I am fully aware of the deep concern felt by the Honourable Member in many matters above his comprehension.'

❋

'Politics is like waking up in the morning. You never know whose head you'll find on the pillow.'

Having been interrupted time and again by one particular Member during a speech to the Commons, Churchill eventually announced, 'The honourable gentleman . . . has arrogated to himself a function which did not belong to him, namely to make my speech instead of letting me make it.'

Terminological diversions:
Words

Churchill's love of words revealed itself above all in the way he enjoyed playing with them. On one occasion it ensured that he lost a game of golf. Violet Bonham-Carter described a round of golf he was playing against her father, the Prime Minister Herbert Asquith. Churchill, who could play a good game when not diverted – but was easily diverted – was well ahead of Asquith until he spotted a shrub with orange berries. Violet Asquith, as she then was, told him it was buckthorn, 'the olive of the north'. 'He rose,' she wrote, 'like a trout to the fly of any phrase and his attention was immediately arrested and deflected from the game. "The olive of the north – that's good. The buckthorn of the south – that's not so good" and during the remaining holes he rang the changes on every possible combination and permutation of this meagre theme, which took his mind and eye completely off the ball.' To Asquith's delight Churchill didn't hit another ball that afternoon and lost the game.

✳

During his long life, Churchill – as a boy noted for failing exams – received many honorary degrees. In 1946, at the University of Miami, on being awarded his doctorate of law, he remarked, with a neat allusion to a famous line he'd uttered some six years before: 'Perhaps no one has ever passed so few examinations and received so many degrees.'

'Men will forgive a man anything except bad prose.' It sounds more as though Churchill were referring to himself here, in his election speech in Manchester, 1906.

*

In one of the many documents that came WSC's way, a civil servant had gone out of his way to be grammatically correct, and had clumsily avoided ending a sentence with a preposition. Churchill scribbled in the margin: 'This is the sort of English up with which I will not put.'

*

'We must have a better word than "prefabricated". Why not "ready-made"?' he complained another time. He was, however, happy to use polysyllabic terms himself on occasion – the difference being that it was often in a spirit of lightheartedness, irony or condescension. In 1906, referring to the government's denials of the exploitation of Chinese coolies in South Africa, he said, 'Perhaps we have been guilty of some terminological inexactitudes.'

*

'Short words are best and the old words when short are best of all.'

As is clear from the sections on politics and friends, it is not only terminological inexactitudes that flew (and fly) around the House of Commons. It is a happy hunting ground for the collectors of insults, and WSC once remarked: 'I do not think any expression of scorn or severity which I have heard used by our critics has come anywhere near the language I have been myself accustomed to use, not only orally, but in a stream of written minutes. In fact, I wonder that a great many of my colleagues are on speaking terms with me.'

✻

There is a story that an American general once asked Churchill to look over the draft of an address he had written. It was returned with the comment 'Too many passives and too many zeds.' The general asked him what he meant, and was told: 'Too many Latinate polysyllabics like "systematize", "prioritize" and "finalize". And then the passives. What if I had said, instead of "We shall fight on the beaches", "Hostilities will be engaged with our adversary on the coastal perimeter"?'

✻

'*The Times* is speechless and takes three columns to express its speechlessness.' (This was on the issue of Irish Home Rule.)

Legend has it that on one occasion, as Churchill was addressing the House of Commons, a Member of Parliament called Wilfred Paling stood up and shouted, 'You dirty dog!' The rejoinder was swift and inevitable: 'Yes. And the Honourable Member should remember what dirty dogs do to palings!'

WSC, always appreciative of words, enjoyed people's names, even if he might sometimes have given some cause for offence. As last of the so-called Hanging Judges, Rayner Goddard (Lord Chief Justice 1946–58) became 'Lord Goddamn'. While, at the Admiralty, Churchill's principal Private Secretary was called Eric Seal, appropriately enough, and it gave Churchill much pleasure to be able to ask a secretary to 'Fetch Seal from his ice-floe'. And when the name of Sir Alfred Bossom came up, his comment was: 'Bossom? What an extraordinary name. Neither one thing nor the other!'

And Admiral Sir Dudley Pound had a name that could be played with . . . on receiving a report from the Admiral with which he did not agree, Churchill wrote under Pound's signature: 'Penny wise'.

✳

'The essential structure of the ordinary British sentence . . . is a noble thing.'

'I think "No comment" is a splendid expression. I am using it again and again. I got it from Sumner Welles,' WSC informed reporters at Washington airport as he was leaving after a conference at the White House with President Truman in February 1946. (Sumner Welles, the American diplomat and writer, was US Under-Secretary of State 1937–42.)

✳

General Sir Henry Maitland Wilson – 'Jumbo' – C-in-C, Middle East, was selected in September 1943 to take the Greek island of Leros with a comparatively small number of troops. 'This is the time to play high,' WSC encouraged him. 'Improvise and dare.' Later he wrote of the General: 'He improvose and dore.'

✳

During the war, at a time when British shipping losses were particularly heavy, both the press and the BBC solemnly reiterated and emphasized the many reports of losses. In a memo to the Admiralty Churchill complained wearily: 'Must we have this lugubrious ingemination of the news of our shipping losses?'

Baffled Admiralty staff, thinking his secretary must have mistyped 'insemination', hurried to their dictionaries – to learn that 'ingemination' means 'reiteration'.

Churchill could not resist puns, even when the circumstances perhaps did not call for levity. When on a tour of Africa in 1907, he was informed by a Colonial Governor that venereal disease was spreading at an alarming rate among the 'natives'. 'Ah, Pox Britannica!' Churchill diagnosed.

✻

On the same journey, after a march of over a hundred miles, Churchill turned to his Private Secretary Eddie Marsh and said, 'So fari – so goodi!'

✻

On a Member's statement that economic planning was baloney: 'I should prefer to have an agreed definition of the meaning of "baloney" before I attempt to deal with such a topic.'

'Pigs treat us as equals':
Animals, real
and metaphorical

Although Winston Churchill is, rightly, famed as an orator and his speeches noted for the rolling fluidity of their language and their power to move and inspire, most of them could not be described as wicked or witty, except in so far as there is a kind of wit in the way he uses language – in the metaphors he employs. Interestingly, animals often figure – as allusions but most often as metaphors in his speeches. Churchill liked animals; sometimes he found this difficult to reconcile with his fondness for rich food. Anthony Montague Brown recalled that 'One Christmas he was about to carve a goose. Learning it was one of his own, he put down the knife and fork and said, "I could not possibly eat a bird that I have known socially."'

'Dogs look up to men, cats look down on them, but pigs just treat us as equals.' He kept all of these animals – and others – but perhaps he felt a special affinity with pigs (charming and intelligent creatures that are much maligned): one of his Private Secretaries described being summoned to Churchill's bedroom where the Prime Minister was lying in bed looking like 'a rather nice pig in a silk suit'. Clementine's pet name for him was 'Pig'. (And apparently the KGB's wartime codename for Churchill was 'Boar' . . . not exactly unbreakable.) In Britain, during the war, however, he was depicted as a bulldog – seen as the 'British Bulldog', epitomizing the never-let-go, never-give-in spirit of the nation.

With his liking for words including the silliest of puns, Churchill called the henhouse he had built for his chickens 'Chickenham Palace'. (Perhaps he was thinking of its residents when he exclaimed 'Some chicken! Some neck!' – words quoted elsewhere in this book.)

*

'Although it may be very difficult to define in law what is or what is not a trade union,' he remarked in the House of Commons in 1911, 'most people of common sense know a trade union when they see one. It is like trying to define a rhinoceros: it is difficult enough, but if one is seen, everybody can recognize it.'

*

'The whipped jackal, who, to save his own skin, has made of Italy a vassal state of Hitler's Empire, is frisking up by the side of the German tiger with yelps not only of appetite – that could be understood – but even of triumph.' (The jackal in this speech to the House in April 1941 is Mussolini. In November 1942 Mussolini transmogrified slightly: 'The hyena in his nature broke all bounds of decency and even common sense.')

On his appointment as First Lord of the Admiralty, Churchill described his pleasure with a rather comical metaphor – especially when one tries to visualize him as a 'fruitful hen' – or imagine poached admirals: 'This is because I can now lay eggs instead of scratching around in the dust and clucking. It is a far more satisfactory occupation. I am at present in process of laying a great number of eggs – "good eggs" every one of them. And there will be many more clutches to follow . . . New appointments to be made. Admirals to be "poached", "scrambled" and "buttered". A fresh egg from a fruitful hen.'

✳

'Dictators ride to and fro upon tigers which they dare not dismount. And the tigers are getting hungry.' In this warning letter of 11 November 1937 Churchill's reference is to the proverb 'He who rides a tiger is afraid to dismount.' (And he must have known the limerick: 'There was a young lady of Riga/Who went for a ride on a tiger; They returned from the ride/With the lady inside,/And a smile on the face of the tiger.' Probably in the English rather than the Latin version.)

'It was the nation and the race dwelling all round the globe that had the lion's heart. I had the luck to be called upon to give the roar. I also hope that I sometimes suggested to the lion the right place to use his claws.' (Speech, 1954.)

✳

'We are waiting for the long-promised invasion. So are the fishes,' Churchill assured the French in a radio broadcast in October 1940. By then, thanks in large measure to the Battle of Britain, Hitler had abandoned his plans for Operation Sealion, the codeword for a German invasion of the British Isles.

✳

'Learn to get used to it. Eels get used to skinning.' These words, dating from 1940, were from a speech delivered in secret session – had they been public, there would have been something of an outcry as the 'it' people were meant to get used to was, apparently, being bombed. He also used the metaphor in referring to caricature: 'Just as eels are supposed to get used to skinning, so politicians get used to being caricatured . . . If we must confess it, they are quite offended and downcast when the cartoons stop.'

Sometimes Churchill encountered problems with animals – notably camels, which are not the most accommodating of creatures. However, Churchill could be as obstinate as them. Edward Marsh remembered a journey to Aden when WSC, as Under-Secretary for the Colonies, asked to have a camel from the camel battery. The battery officer – deliberately? – produced one known to be bad-tempered and prone to kicking. A Somali boy later reported to the officer: 'Effendi, effendi, camel kick Churchill; Churchill kick camel. Him very good camel now, effendi.'

In 1921, Churchill, then Colonial Secretary, and his companions were crossing the desert on camels. Suddenly his saddle slipped round and dumped WSC unceremoniously in the sand. A number of Bedouin accompanying the group immediately dashed up to him, each offering his horse. But: 'I started on a camel and I will finish on a camel,' declared Churchill.

✳

'We are all worms. But I do believe that I am a glow-worm,' he remarked to Violet Bonham-Carter, no doubt bringing to an early end a philosophic discussion of life, the universe and everything.

'An appeaser is one who feeds a crocodile – hoping that it will eat him last.' Elsewhere, as we have seen, he remarks that 'Trying to maintain good relations with a Communist is like wooing a crocodile.'

✳

'We hoped to land a wildcat that would tear out the bowels of the Boche. Instead we have stranded a vast whale with its tail flopping about in the water!' This dramatic picture is a reference to the US and British combined landing at Anzio on the west coast of Italy, which was almost thrown back by the Germans, with high casualties.

Casting pearls:
Speeches

Making speeches, WSC is said to have claimed, is 'The art of making deep sounds from the stomach sound like important messages from the brain.' It is a great deal more than this, of course, as Churchill well knew. His friend Lord Birkenhead's quip, 'Winston has devoted the best years of his life to preparing his impromptu speeches', carries more than a grain of truth. Unlike many, if not most, statesmen, Churchill did not employ a speechwriter – he worked hard preparing his speeches, usually in bed, often remarking of those that were taking a lot of effort, 'This speech is hanging over me like a vulture.' He would also sometimes say, 'I'm going to make a long speech because I've not had the time to prepare a short one,' which is not as illogical as it sounds, as anyone who has had to condense an argument into a limited number of words will recognize. He also said of verbosity, 'it is sheer laziness not compressing thought into a reasonable space'.

✳

One of Churchill's most famous speeches is that of June 1940: 'We shall fight on the beaches, we shall fight on the landing grounds, we shall fight in the fields and in the streets, we shall fight in the hills . . .' It is said that, as he paused in the great uproar that greeted these words, Churchill muttered to a colleague next to him, 'And we'll fight them with the butt ends of broken beer bottles because that's bloody well all we've got!'

'Call that a maiden speech? I call it a brazen hussy of a speech.' The novelist, humorist, lawyer and politician A. P. Herbert recalled Churchill's view of an overconfident first address to the House of Commons, recorded in Leslie Frewin's 1973 Churchill compilation, *Immortal Jester*.

✳

The Chamber had – as always when he was about to speak – filled up with MPs, to whom Churchill delivered a masterful and forceful speech. At the end of it a disgruntled Member remarked 'Here endeth the book of Jeremiah'; his neighbour watched all the MPs flock out now that the speech was over and added 'Followed, I see, by Exodus.'

✳

Churchill's opinion of the admiral and intermittent MP Lord Charles Beresford (given in a speech to the House of Commons in 1912) as an orator gives us a taste of his firm views on public speaking. It is worth noting, however, that Beresford was one of those who made very clear his opposition to Churchill's election as a Member of Parliament. 'He is one of those orators,' WSC snorted, 'of whom it was well said, "Before they get up, they do not know what they are going to say; when they are speaking, they do not know what they are saying; and when they have sat down, they do not know what they have said." '

During a long and boring speech from one of the many less inspiring MPs, Churchill spotted an elderly Member straining with an ear trumpet to hear what was being said, and demanded loudly, 'Who is that fool denying his natural advantages?'

✳

'I can well understand the Honourable Member's wishing to speak on. He needs the practice badly.'

✳

Asked – unwisely – by a young MP how he could have put more fire into the speech he had just made, Churchill's alleged answer was predictable: 'What you should have done is put the speech into the fire.'

✳

When another Member of Parliament remarked to Churchill on the fact that he never began an address with the words 'It is a pleasure to . . .', Churchill answered, 'It may be an honour, but never a pleasure. There are only a few things from which I derive intense pleasure, and speaking is not one of them.'

A BBC broadcaster described once sitting next to Churchill as he gave a speech, keeping his audience hanging on to his every word. The broadcaster noticed, however, that what appeared to be notes in Churchill's hand was only a laundry slip, and he later remarked upon this to Churchill. 'Yes,' said WSC. 'It gave confidence to my audience.'

✳

'Let us not shrink from using the short expressive phrase even if it is conversational.' Two of Churchill's most famous speeches made use of colloquial exclamations, to good effect.

In a speech in Ottawa, 1941 – 'When I warned them [the French] that Britain would fight on alone whatever they did, their generals told their Prime Minister and his divided Cabinet: "In three weeks England will have her neck wrung like a chicken." Some chicken! Some neck!'

('Some chicken! Some neck' aroused laughter and applause not only for its spirited language, but also because, unknown to him at the time, 'neck' in Canada was slang for 'nerve'.)

And in a speech to the US Congress in December that same year (referring to the Japanese, and quoted later): 'What kind of people do they think we are?'

Many speakers in the House of Commons liked to adorn their speeches with Latin tags – most of them could, after all, understand Latin – at least, most of those who had the advantage of a public school education . . . Churchill, on the other hand, usually stuck to the English language. On one occasion, however, he did include a quotation in Latin: '. . . which I will now proceed to translate for the benefit of those . . .' he paused. The Labour members, hackles beginning to rise, waited to hear 'lacking the advantage of a public school education', to be completely deflated as, smiling benignly, the Prime Minister repeated, 'For the benefit . . . of any Old Etonians who may be present.'

✳

Churchill enjoyed teasing his audience in the House of Commons and – as the stuff of parliamentary speeches can sometimes be pretty heavy going – no doubt the gathered MPs looked forward to his speeches partly for this very reason.

'Of course it is perfectly possible for honourable members to prevent my speaking, and indeed I do not want to cast my pearls before . . .' he conceded one day, pausing as the entire House waited expectantly for 'swine', '. . . those who do not want them.'

(They no doubt knew that Churchill was fond of pigs.)

Friends like these . . .

'I hate nobody except Hitler – and that is professional.' If one were to judge by the following, however, one would suppose Churchill, his fellow politicians and the military leaders were the bitterest of enemies. Some, it is true, he liked, and they liked him, whatever their politics. Others – such as the Welsh Labour MP, Aneurin Bevan – he did not like. Whether or not they liked one another, however, was no obstacle to the insults they threw at each other.

＊

Military leaders could find their Prime Minister and his interference in their conduct of the war exasperating to say the least, as two Chiefs of the Imperial General Staff were to record. According to *Field Marshal Sir Henry Wilson*, referring to Churchill at the time of the Great War, 'His judgement is always at fault, and he is hopeless when in power.'

Field Marshal Lord Alanbrooke (General Sir Alan Brooke), CIGS during much of the Second World War, was of much the same opinion: 'He [WSC] knows no details, has only got half the picture in his mind, talks absurdities and makes my blood boil to listen to his nonsense . . . And the wonderful thing is that ¾ of the population of the world imagine Winston Churchill is one of the great Strategists of History, a second Marlborough, and the other ¼ have no conception of what a public menace he is.' (He also said, on other occasions, 'Winston is a marvel. I can't imagine how he sticks it', 'He is quite the most wonderful man I have ever met, and is a source of never-ending interest to me', and 'He is the most difficult man I have ever served, but thank god for having given me the opportunity.')

✳

And *Churchill on Alanbrooke*: 'When I thump the table and push my face towards him, what does he do? Thumps the table harder and glares back at me.'

✳

Evelyn Waugh is said to have described Churchill as 'simply a radio personality who outlived his prime'.

✳

Lady Lugard, the knowledgeable and distinguished wife of the Governor of Hong Kong, was of the opinion that Churchill was 'an ignorant boy, so obviously ignorant in regard to colonial affairs and at the same time so full of personal activity that the damage he may do appears to be colossal.' WSC was at the time Under-Secretary for the Colonies.

The great advocate and wit *Lord Birkenhead (F. E. Smith)*, was known to have been a good friend of Churchill's, but that did not prevent him from exercising his sharp tongue just a little at his friend's expense: 'Mr Churchill,' he once remarked, 'is easily satisfied with the best.' He also said: 'When Winston is right he is unique. When he is wrong—Oh my God!' And on another occasion: 'Winston has devoted the best years of his life to preparing his impromptu speeches.'

✳

Margot Asquith, Herbert Asquith's second wife, found his vanity a bit much at times, and is said on one occasion to have exclaimed: 'He would kill his own mother just so that he could use her skin to make a drum to beat his own praises.'

And in a strongly worded letter to Balfour in 1916 – at a time when tempers were running high following a dramatic and ill-considered speech by Churchill in which he systematically demolished the Admiralty he had recently had to leave – she called him 'a hound of the lowest sense of political honour, a fool of the lowest judgement & contemptible. He cured me of oratory in the House & bored me with oratory in the Home!' She never did get on with Churchill.

WSC on the Duke of Windsor
Although Churchill allowed his sentimental side to take sway and supported Edward VIII in his desire to marry Mrs Simpson, on another occasion he described him as 'A little man dressed up to the nines'. In fact, Churchill was more than usually inconsistent in his view of the crisis occasioned by the King's love for an American divorcée. On one occasion he remarked to Colville that he thought the love affair was merely one of Edward VIII's temporary infatuations, and on another described it as 'one of the great love stories in history'.

✳

WSC on Lord Macaulay
'It is beyond our hopes to overtake Lord Macaulay ... We can only hope that Truth will follow swiftly enough to fasten the label "Liar" to his genteel coat-tails.' Churchill as a historian himself ensured that his subjects were thoroughly researched and did not allow flights of the imagination. In his biography of his forebear, *Marlborough*, he sought to defend the Duke of Marlborough against Macaulay's claims.

✳

WSC on Joseph Chamberlain (a Liberal, later Conservative, statesman, father of Austen and Neville)
'Mr Chamberlain loves the working man; he loves to see him work.'

'The country thought Mr Chamberlain . . . was a prophet with a message. They found him a politician groping for a platform.'

✳

WSC on Austen Chamberlain (like his father and half-brother, a statesman; he was twice Chancellor of the Exchequer and, in 1921, leader of the Conservative party)
'He always played the game and he always lost it.'

✳

WSC on Arthur Balfour (Conservative politician, and Prime Minister 1902–6)
'If you wanted nothing done, Arthur Balfour was the best man for the task. There was no equal to him.'

'He would very soon have put Socrates in his place, if that old fellow had played any of his dialectical tricks on him. When I go to Heaven, I shall try to arrange a chat between these two on some topic not too recondite for me to follow.'

'The dignity of a prime minister, like a lady's virtue, is not susceptible of partial diminution.'
 WSC was commenting on Prime Minister Balfour's efforts to disassociate himself from the contending factions within his party.

And Balfour, in 1899, on WSC
'I thought he was a young man of promise; but it appears he is a young man of promises.'

✳

WSC on Stanley Baldwin
'The Government cannot make up their minds, or they cannot get the Prime Minister to make up his mind,' Churchill wrote of Stanley Baldwin's government in 1936. 'So they go on, in strange paradox, decided only to be undecided, resolved to be irresolute, adamant for drift, solid for fluidity, all-powerful to be impotent.'

Asked to send an eightieth birthday letter to Baldwin, Churchill declined: 'I wish Stanley Baldwin no ill, but it would have been much better if he had never lived.' He had perhaps forgotten that it was Baldwin who had given him the post of Chancellor of the Exchequer in 1924, an appointment which had delighted him and filled him with great excitement.

'In those days Mr Baldwin was wiser than he is now; he used frequently to take my advice.' 'Those days' were presumably the latter years of the 1920s, after Baldwin had appointed Churchill Chancellor of the Exchequer – now, in 1935 and in the wilderness, Churchill's obsessive concern was Britain's lack of preparedness for war and the government's lack of preparedness to listen to him.

'He has his ear so close to the ground that he has locusts in it.'

'It is a fine thing to be honest, but it is also very important to be right.' Clearly, Churchill felt that Baldwin's adherence to honesty did not necessarily help him to perceive the broader truth.

And, distinguishing truth from honesty, Churchill also said of him: 'He occasionally stumbled over the truth, but hastily picked himself up and hurried on as if nothing had happened.' Interestingly, Baldwin said that Churchill 'cannot really tell lies. That is what makes him so bad a conspirator.'

'One never hears of Baldwin nowadays – he might as well be dead,' someone remarked. 'No,' answered Churchill, 'not dead. But the candle in that great turnip has gone out.' This exchange was recorded in Harold Nicolson's diary for August 1950. Baldwin died in 1947.

✳

WSC on Ramsay MacDonald (Britain's first Labour Prime Minister)
'I remember, when I was a child, being taken to the celebrated Barnum's Circus, which contained an exhibition of freaks and monstrosities, but the exhibition on the programme which I most desired to see was one described as the "Boneless Wonder".

My parents judged that spectacle would be too revolting and demoralizing for my young eyes, and I have waited fifty years to see the "Boneless Wonder" on the Treasury Bench.' (These words, in a speech of January 1931, referred to MacDonald's indecisiveness on trade union reform.)

'The greatest living master of falling without hurting himself.' (The government has just been defeated by 30 votes, in January 1931, and the PM, Ramsay MacDonald, rises 'utterly unabashed . . . and airily assures us that nothing has happened'.)

'We know that he has, more than any other man, the gift of compressing the largest amount of words into the smallest amount of thought.'

✳

WSC on Lord Esher (Reginald Baliol Brett, 2nd Viscount Esher, government official, courtier and diarist, and Liberal MP)
'We must conclude that an uncontrollable fondness for fiction forbade him to forsake it for fact. Such constancy is a defect in an historian.' (On Lord Esher's description of Churchill's part in the Antwerp operation in September 1914.) Churchill had taken it upon himself to organize the defence of the Belgian port, a vain effort in the event, and one that cost the Royal Naval Division dear. Although elsewhere Churchill implied that he didn't mind

criticism, he also admitted to being an egoist – and don't most egoists mind being criticized, when, that is, they notice that they are being criticized?

✳

WSC on Neville Chamberlain (son of Joseph Chamberlain, and Conservative Prime Minister, 1937–40; Churchill was very critical of his policy of appeasement)
'An old town clerk looking at European affairs through the wrong end of a municipal drainpipe.' Chamberlain had once been Mayor of Birmingham.

'He has a lust for peace.'

'You were given the choice between war and dishonour. You chose dishonour and you will have war.' These words, bitter and true, were spoken just after the Munich settlement of 29 September 1938.

'In the depths of that dusty soul there is nothing but abject surrender.'

A few months after Chamberlain's return from Munich, waving his famous piece of paper, in 1938, during a debate on Palestine, Malcolm MacDonald, Secretary of State for the Colonies, had reached the end of a difficult speech and was discoursing lyrically about the land itself: 'Bethlehem, where the Prince of Peace was born . . .' he intoned, to be interrupted by Churchill's voice: '"Bethlehem"? I thought Neville was born in Birmingham.'

When someone remarked that Chamberlain, in his effort to make Attlee (leader of the Labour Party; Prime Minister, 1945–51) accept the Munich appeasement, resembled a snake dominating a rabbit, Churchill countered, 'It's more like a rabbit dominating a lettuce!'

Early in 1939 the Duchess of Buccleuch had Churchill over one weekend. As he was leaving she asked him if he could advise her: Neville Chamberlain was coming the next weekend to address the local Conservatives. Where should she set up the podium? 'It doezhn't matter where you put it, as long as he hazh the shun in hizh eyes and the wind in hizh teeth.'

(Chamberlain died in 1940, not long after resigning, having fought a hard and uncomplaining battle against cancer. Churchill, now Prime Minister, was profoundly moved and spoke generously of his predecessor in the Commons: 'The only guide to a man is his conscience; the only shield to his memory is the rectitude and sincerity of his actions.')

WSC on Field Marshal Sir Bernard Montgomery
(1st Viscount Montgomery of Alamein, one of
Britain's most successful military leaders)
'In defeat, unbeatable; in victory, unbearable.'
(A variation of this is sometimes attributed to
Churchill, again as a description of Montgomery:
'Indomitable in retreat, invincible in advance,
insufferable in victory'.) Churchill was fond of
Montgomery, though, and Monty remained a faithful friend to the end, visiting him at Chartwell – not
necessarily by invitation – where the two old men
sat together and exchanged reminiscences over tea
and other things.

In 1960, not long after the attempt to overthrow the
Panama government, in which Margot Fonteyn's
husband, Tito Arias, had taken part and for which
he had been jailed, they visited the Churchills at
Chartwell. WSC asked Arias what he was going to
do, and Arias told him, 'We shall go back to
Panama.'

'Don't use Montgomery in any of your revolu-
tions,' Churchill advised him. 'He will bankrupt you
before you start. He will need thirteen divisions
before he'll ever make a move!'

During the North Africa campaign, the Eighth
Army captured the Field Commander of the Afrika
Korps, General Wilhelm von Thoma, and General
Montgomery, commanding the Eighth Army,
invited his captive to dine in his GHQ trailer.

This horrified many at home in Britain, but the Prime Minister's reaction was rather more measured. 'I sympathize with General von Thoma,' he remarked. 'Defeated, humiliated, in captivity, and . . . [long pause for dramatic effect] . . . dinner with Montgomery.'

✳

WSC on R. A. (Rab) Butler (Conservative politician, who held important government positions, including that of Chancellor)
'I am amused by the Chancellor of the Exchequer. He is always patting himself on the back, a kind of exercise that contributes to his excellent physical condition.' (And this was the man who put up with Churchill's budgerigar sitting on his head.)

✳

WSC on Charles de Gaulle (French general, leader of the Free French, elected Prime Minister, then President of France, 1958–69)
'He looks like a female llama who has just been surprised in her bath.' (Lord Moran – Sir Charles Wilson, Churchill's doctor – also saw something of the ruminant in the Free French leader, later to be President of France, describing him as 'an improbable creature, like a human giraffe, sniffing down his nostrils at mortals beneath his gaze.')

WSC on Field Marshal Lord Kitchener (military leader and statesman; Secretary of State for War, 1914 to his death in 1916)

'He may be a general but never a gentleman.' (Poor 'K' – whose recruiting campaign in 1914 did so much to prepare the British Army for the long agony of the Great War – inspired little liking. The ever sharp-tongued *Margot Asquith* remarked of him: 'If Kitchener was not a great man, he was, at least, a great poster.')

✳

WSC on Aneurin (Nye) Bevan

'He will be as great a curse to this country in peace as he was a squalid nuisance in time of war.'

'I can think of no better step to signal the inauguration of the National Health Service than that a person who so obviously needs psychiatric attention should be among the first of its patients.'

'A merchant of discourtesy.'

'If you recognize anyone, it does not mean that you like him. We all, for instance, recognize the honourable Member for Ebbw Vale.' These words, in a speech of July 1952, were in reference to British recognition of communist China. The Member in question was Nye Bevan.

Nye Bevan on WSC
'He is a man suffering from petrified adolescence.'

'I welcome this opportunity of pricking the bloated bladder of lies with the poniard of truth.'

'He never spares himself in conversation. He gives himself so generously that hardly anybody else is permitted to give anything in his presence.'

*

WSC on Clement Attlee
'A sheep in sheep's clothing.'

'If any grub is fed on Royal Jelly it turns into a Queen Bee.'

'He is a modest man who has a good deal to be modest about.'

'An empty taxi arrived at 10 Downing Street, and when the door was opened Attlee got out. ' (This wisecrack, doing the rounds of Westminster shortly after the war, was ascribed to Churchill. When, however, his friend and Private Secretary Jock Colville repeated it and its attribution to him, Churchill's face stiffened and 'after an awful pause', he said: 'Mr Attlee is an honourable and gallant gentleman, and a faithful colleague who served his country well at the time of her greatest need. I should be obliged if you would make it clear whenever an occasion arises that I would never make such a remark about him, and that I strongly disapprove of anybody who does.' The vehemence and pomposity of this denial suggest that perhaps Churchill *was* responsible for the jest, but, whether as a matter of conscience or for some other personal reason, was immediately anxious to disown it. Attlee had been Leader of the House of Commons in Churchill's coalition government, and indeed Churchill had deputed day-to-day business to him. He seems to have been anxious not to hurt Attlee unnecessarily – although it's unclear whether this is because he liked him, or because Attlee was particularly easy to hurt, or for some other reason. When he left office in 1945, giving up his post to Attlee, he took leave of his Private Secretary Paul Beards, with the assurance: 'Mr Attlee is a very nice man.')

Attlee on WSC
'Fifty per cent of Winston is genius, fifty per cent bloody fool. He *will* behave like a child.'

✳

WSC on Lloyd George (Liberal statesman, PM 1916–22, and friend of Churchill)
'The Happy Warrior of Squandermania.'

WSC on Herbert Morrison (Labour statesman, and deputy PM in Attlee's administration, 1945–51)
'A curious mixture of geniality and venom.'

✳

WSC on his friend Lord Beaverbrook (Max Aitken, a Canadian Scot who became a Conservative MP; and later a newspaper mogul)
'He is a foul-weather friend.'

Beaverbrook on WSC
'Churchill has the habit of breaking the rungs of any ladder he puts his foot on.'

✳

WSC on US President Woodrow Wilson
'The spacious philanthropy which he exhaled upon Europe stopped quite sharply on the coasts of his own country.' Woodrow Wilson tried to maintain the neutrality of the United States following the outbreak of the First World War, and succeeded uncomfortably until 1917. After the war he fought hard to set up the League of Nations, the ineffectual forebear of the United Nations, concentrating on it to the extent that he took his eye off his political affairs in the United States, where Republican opposition to his peacekeeping plans for Europe was building up.

WSC on Hitler
'If Hitler invaded Hell I would make at least a favourable reference to the Devil in the House of Commons.' (This was in fact an allusion to Hitler having invaded Russia. Churchill, having often spoken vociferously against the Soviet regime over the years, was now prepared to helping Russia. On the subjects of hell and Russia, Churchill once remarked to Leo Amery that God must exist because of 'the existence of Lenin and Trotsky for whom a hell is needed'.)

✳

WSC on the Russian Foreign Minister Vyacheslav Mikhailovich Molotov:
'I have never seen a human being who more perfectly represented the modern concept of a robot.'

✳

WSC on T. E. Lawrence
'He was not in complete harmony with the normal.'

'He has a way of backing into the limelight' – this is usually attributed to Lord Berners ('He's always backing into the limelight'), from whom Churchill may well have borrowed the neat turn of phrase.

WSC on Stafford Cripps (Labour statesman, Chancellor of the Exchequer 1947–50)

It was probably not so much Stafford Cripps's politics (after all, he had been expelled from the Labour Party for opposing appeasement, which must have earned WSC's approval) that got up Churchill's nose as his almost inhuman austerity. Deeply religious, severely honest and sincere, and, naturally, a teetotaller, he was an uncomfortable figure to have around for someone like Churchill, who was shameless in his indulgence in luxury and drink; indeed, as Jock Colville put it, Cripps 'was also suspected of believing that the hair shirts which he chose for his own wardrobe should be manufactured and distributed to the whole community'. Apparently, however, he allowed himself one luxury – smoking cigars – until he forswore that, too, announcing the move as an example of the kind of wartime sacrifice expected of the nation.

On hearing this, Churchill mumbled to a colleague, 'Too bad – that was his last contact with humanity.'

'He has all the virtues I dislike and none of the vices I admire.'

Seated opposite this paragon of righteousness at dinner, Churchill suddenly remarked: 'I am glad I am not a herbivore. I eat what I like, I drink what I like, I do what I like . . . and *he's* the one to have a red nose.'

'There but for the grace of God goes God.'

'His chest is a cage in which two squirrels are at war – his conscience and his career.'

'He delivers his speech with an expression of injured guilt.'

In December 1940 Cripps was British Ambassador to the Soviet Union, in Churchill's words, 'a lunatic in a country of lunatics'.

✳

WSC on US Secretary of State John Foster Dulles
'He is the only bull I know who carries his own china closet with him.'

'Dull, Duller, Dulles.'

✳

US President Roosevelt on WSC
Roosevelt is reported to have said 'Churchill has a hundred ideas a day, of which four are good ideas.'

WSC on George Bernard Shaw
'Few people practise what they preach and none less
so than George Bernard Shaw . . . Saint, sage and
clown; venerable, profound and irresistible.'

'He was one of my earliest antipathies,' Churchill
wrote in *Great Contemporaries*. 'This bright, nimble,
fierce, and comprehending being – Jack Frost danc-
ing bespangled in the sunshine.'

An exchange of telegrams
GBS: 'Two tickets reserved for you, first night
Pygmalion. Bring a friend. If you have one.'
WSC: 'Cannot make first night. Will come to
second. If you have one.'

'Of course I'm an egoist'

Just before he started to work for Churchill, Pamela Plowden, an early love of Churchill's, told a nervous Eddie Marsh – Churchill's first Private Secretary – that 'The first time you meet Winston you see all his faults, and the rest of your life you spend in discovering his virtues.'

✳

Echoing Pamela Plowden, Field Marshal Sir Henry Wilson said of Churchill, 'He has many good qualities, some of which lie hidden, and he has many bad qualities, all of which are in the shop window.'

✳

'Eating my words has never given me indigestion.'

✳

'I am certainly not one of those who need to be prodded. In fact, if anything, I am a prod.'

✳

Struck down by acute appendicitis during the 1922 election, he lost his seat at Dundee, and was able to say: 'I am without an office, without a seat . . . and without an appendix.'

'I cannot help reflecting that if my father had been an American and my mother British, instead of the other way round, I might have got here on my own.' (Churchill addressing the US Congress, December 1941.)

✳

Field Marshal Sir William Slim (in a discussion of standard rifles for Nato forces in 1952): 'Well, I suppose we could experiment with a bastard rifle – partly American, partly British.'
WSC: 'Kindly moderate your language – it may be recalled that I am myself partly British, partly American.'

✳

'Be on your guard! I'm going to speak in French – a formidable undertaking and one which will put great demands upon your friendship for Great Britain.' (As these words were uttered in a speech at Paris just after the Liberation of France, the French doubtless forgave every distortion of their beloved language from the man who some years later was to say, 'Everybody has a right to pronounce foreign names as he chooses.')

'I am not usually accused even by my friends of a modest or retiring disposition.'

*

'I do not resent criticism, even when, for the sake of emphasis, it parts for the time with reality,' Churchill informed the House of Commons in January 1941.

*

'Madam, all babies look like me.' WSC's response to a woman who came up to him and declared that her baby looked just like him.

*

When, as they travelled across the Atlantic together in 1929, his friend, the journalist and politician Leo Amery, suggested that Churchill might find himself breaking away from the Conservative Party when the party moved back to tariffs and protectionism, WSC replied that 'I shall stick to you with all the loyalty of a leech.'

'I am easily satisfied with the best.' Birkenhead's witticism had pleased Churchill, who adopted it for himself (or maybe he was quoting his friend but forgetting to acknowledge him), and used it more than once. Indeed, there is even a story that on the day that he was due to arrive at the Plaza Hotel in New York for a few days, the manager of the hotel, knowing nothing of Churchill's preferences in food and drink, and anxious to please him, telephoned the British Embassy in Washington. He was just explaining this to the person who answered the telephone when there was an interruption at the other end and a new voice came on the line: 'Yesh?'

'I am the director of the Plaza Hotel inquiring about Mr Churchill's tastes – '

'Mr Churchill,' the voice interrupted him, 'izh a man of simple tashtes – eazhily shatishfied with the besht.'

Churchill also said of himself, echoing Lord Birkenhead's assessment of him, 'I always manage somehow to adjust to any new level of luxury without whimper or complaint. It is one of my more winning traits.' And 'I have in my life concentrated more on self-expression than on self-denial.'

✻

'If I am accused of making this mistake, I can only say with M. Clemenceau on a celebrated occasion, "Perhaps I have made a number of other mistakes of which you have not heard." ' (Georges Clemenceau, the 'Tiger', French statesman, led France through the First World War, and was much admired by Churchill.)

✳

Following the bitter blow of his defeat before the end of the war, WSC was asked to tour the country to give people the opportunity to honour him. He replied, 'I refuse to be exhibited like a prize bull whose chief attraction is his past prowess.'

✳

'I suppose they asked me to show him that, if they couldn't bark themselves, they kept a dog who could bark and might bite,' he commented, on having been invited by Chamberlain to meet Joachim von Ribbentrop, then German Ambassador to Britain.

✳

'It had many defects and teething troubles, and when these became apparent the tank was appropriately rechristened the "Churchill".' The tank in question had been in use for a couple of years or so, but although it had good qualities – it was relatively roomy and virtually unstoppable – it was under-gunned and rather slow. By the time of this speech to the House of Commons in July 1942 improvements had been implemented.

'Unpunctuality is a vile habit, and all my life I have tried to break myself of it.'

✳

'I am a sporting man. I always like to give trains and aeroplanes a fair chance of getting away.'

✳

'I suppress with difficulty an impulse to become sententious. '

✳

'Megalomania is the only form of sanity.' (He said this when, as First Lord of the Admiralty, he began planning large-scale ship-building programmes.)

✳

'All the years that I have been in the House of Commons I have always said to myself one thing: "Do not interrupt" and I have never been able to keep to that resolution.' (Sarah Churchill recalled a noisy family meal in which her father's voice rose above all the others, roaring amid loud laughter, 'Randolph, do stop interrupting me while I'm interrupting you!')

'I am always ready to learn although I do not always like being taught.' (After he had failed twice to get into Sandhurst, the young Winston Churchill was sent to a crammer run by a Captain James, who specialized in getting boys through their army exams: Captain James informed Winston's father that 'He has been rather too much inclined up to the present to teach his instructors instead of endeavouring to learn from them.')

'I am ready to meet my Maker. Whether my Maker is ready for the ordeal of meeting me is another matter,' Churchill pronounced on his seventy-fifth birthday, 30 November 1949.

✳

'Of course I'm an egoist. Where do you get if you aren't?'

✳

In a speech in 1986, Anthony Montague Browne, a former Private Secretary to Winston Churchill, recalled the following exchange:

Sir Samuel Hoare: 'Winston has written a huge book all about himself and called it *The World Crisis*.'
WSC: 'I have not always been wrong. History will bear me out, particularly as I shall write that history myself.'

'Although always prepared for martyrdom, I pre-
ferred that it should be postponed.' He wrote these
words in *My Early Life* of his eventful years fighting
to gain a political foothold (as well as in physical
battles), and one could say that they held true
throughout his life.

✳

At the end of the 1943 Cairo Conference, President
Inönü of Turkey gave WSC a farewell embrace. He
drew Eden's attention to this but Eden was unim-
pressed, commenting that it was little enough
exchange for fifteen hours' hard argument. That
night WSC said to his daughter Sarah, 'Do you
know what happened to me today? The Turkish
President kissed me. The truth is I'm irresistible.
But don't tell Anthony – he's jealous.' (Eden was
Foreign Secretary at the time; he was to succeed
Churchill as Prime Minister in 1955.)

✳

In a letter to Margot Asquith, he once wrote, 'The
world is not made up of heroes and heroines – luckily or where would you and I find our backgrounds!'
As they usually rubbed each other up the wrong
way, the comment is probably directed against her,
his assumption being that many would deny that he
was not a hero.

When he went to a dinner for the Prince of Wales, later Edward VII, in 1896, Churchill wrote later, 'I realized that I must be on my best behaviour – punctual, subdued, reserved – in short, display all the qualities with which I am the least endowed.'

✳

Considering the world and its occupants, Churchill once mused: 'I wonder what God thinks of the things His creatures have invented. Really, it's surprising He has allowed it – but then I suppose He has so many things to think of, not only us, but all His worlds. I wouldn't have his job for anything. Mine is hard enough, but his is much more difficult. And – umph – He can't even resign . . .'

✳

After the First World War, Churchill was awarded the American Distinguished Service Cross for providing the United States with munitions (he became Minister of Munitions in 1917, the year in which the USA entered the war). He explained to a friend that the award was usually presented 'for distinguished service and gallantry in the face of the enemy,' and continued: 'The latter qualification was waived in my case.'

'My idea of a good dinner is, first to have good food, then discuss good food, and after this good food has been elaborately discussed, to discuss a good topic – with me as chief conversationalist.'

✳

At the age of eighty-seven Churchill broke his left thigh in a fall in Monte Carlo. On his return to London, as he was being carried over the threshold by an ambulance attendant, he exhorted him: 'Not feet first, please!'

✳

Asked what he thought about death and the after-life, WSC answered, 'Some kind of velvety cool blackness. Of course, I admit I may be wrong. It is conceivable that I might well be reborn as a Chinese coolie. In such a case I should lodge a protest.' (On another occasion, however, he said, 'Everyone will have equal rights in Heaven. That will be the real Welfare State . . .')

What kind of people?':
The nations according to Churchill

'The English never draw a line without blurring it.'

✳

'Frightfulness is not a remedy known to the British pharmacopoeia.' This comment was provoked by the infamous Amritsar massacre, where General Dyer did employ frightfulness, in ordering his men to fire into an unarmed crowd packed into a large walled enclosure.

✳

On one occasion when he was Prime Minister, Churchill had a brief meeting with his counterpart in the Republic of Ireland at a time when both countries were facing serious problems. When Churchill remarked to the Irish PM that, in his view, the situation in the United Kingdom was serious but not hopeless, the Irish Prime Minister replied – according to Churchill – that the situation in *his* country was hopeless but not serious.

✳

'There are few virtues that the Poles do not possess – and there are few errors they have ever avoided,' he said to the House in 1945.

'Here we have a state whose subjects are so happy that they have to be forbidden to quit its bounds under the direst penalties; whose diplomatists and agents sent on foreign missions have often to leave their wives and children at home to ensure their eventual return,' Churchill said of Russia in 1919.

✳

And in 1942: 'Everybody has always underrated the Russians. They keep their own secrets alike from foe and friends.'

✳

It is said that at the Yalta conference in 1945, Roosevelt having made a fulsome tribute to the Soviet leader, Churchill was persuaded by an aide to follow suit (objecting the while: 'But they do not want peace'). Getting to his feet, he proposed a toast to 'Premier Stalin, whose conduct of foreign policy manifests a desire for peace.' Then, in a whispered aside out of the interpreter's hearing: 'A piece of Poland, a piece of Czechoslovakia, a piece of Romania . . .'

✳

'In Russia a man is called reactionary if he objects to having his property stolen and his wife and children murdered.'

During a Canadian press interview following a tour of the United States in the 1930s, Churchill was asked if he had any complaints about America: 'Toilet paper too thin, newspapers too fat.'

✳

'The Almighty in His infinite wisdom did not see fit to create Frenchmen in the image of Englishmen,' Churchill informed the House of Commons in 1942.

✳

After the First World War, Churchill was in France to give a speech – which he began to do in French. The French, however, found it too difficult to follow his pronunciation so called upon an interpreter to translate. When the interpreter had delivered a magnificently flowery-sounding speech, the audience burst into applause. WSC was temporarily discomfited – whose speech was it, anyway? – but recovered his aplomb rapidly and turned to the translator to declare, in French: 'Until I heard your splendid version, Monsieur, I did not realize what a magnificent, indeed epoch-making, speech I had made. Allow me to embrace you, Monsieur.'

This he did, kissing the interpreter firmly on both cheeks, to redoubled applause.

'Si vous m'obstaclerez, je vous liquiderai,' Churchill delivered fiercely to a startled de Gaulle during negotiations at Casablanca. His attitude towards speaking foreign languages was idiosyncratic.

Complaining, in 1940, of the lack of unity in the French government and the precious time this was wasting, he baffled a French guest by announcing, 'Nous allons perdre l'omnibus.' He may well have been echoing Chamberlain's unhappy remark on 7 April that year that Hitler had 'missed the bus'. Two days later Germany invaded Denmark and Norway, thus inaugurating the Nazi conquest of a large part of Continental Europe.

✳

'For good or for ill the French people have been effective masters in their own house, and have built as they chose upon the ruins of the old regime. Their difficulty is to like what they have done,' Churchill wrote in 1936.

✳

'It becomes still more difficult to reconcile Japanese action with prudence or even sanity. What kind of people do they think we are?' Churchill asked rhetorically in a speech to the US Congress in December 1941, some two to three weeks after the Japanese 'declaration of war', i.e. the attack on the US Pacific Fleet in Pearl Harbor.

And the following January he alluded in the House of Commons to 'The Japanese, whose game is what I may call to make hell while the sun shines . . .'

✻

It is said that in 1943 Churchill sent Anthony Eden on a mission to bring Turkey into the war. In due course he received a telegram from Eden: 'Progress slow. What more can I tell Turkey?' At which Churchill commented: 'Tell them Christmas is coming!'

✻

'India is a geographical term. It is no more a united nation than the Equator.'

Henpecked?:
Women and the family

Churchill was probably typical of his time in his attitude towards the family, women, and women's rights. He had been brought up to believe that the women ran the household, tended the husband and bore and looked after children. Family life and motherhood, he once claimed, 'must be the fountain spring of present happiness and future survival'. His pronouncement 'You must have four children. One for Mother, one for Father, one for Accidents, one for Increase' has a very Victorian ring to it – although it could have been uttered tongue-in-cheek.Women were not inferior beings but they were different beings, and he could not see the point of giving women the vote – their husbands or fathers handled that side of life for them. He at first found the idea of women's suffrage hard to accept – being particularly put off by violent demonstrations – and just as he was coming round to the idea – 'I am anxious to see women relieved in principle from a disability which is injurious to them,' he wrote – he was almost pushed under a train by an angry suffragette in 1909 and had to be rescued by his wife. It was not until 1918 that women got the vote (those over thirty, the age lowered to twenty-one ten years later). He would probably have said that, at home, his wife Clementine ruled supreme – most of the time.

Other women in his life included his secretaries. He worked them hard – to the point of making them stay up all night taking dictation – ('I shall need two women tonight' he would say to his

Private Secretary at busy times, no doubt loudly enough to startle any guest not in the know); and he was kind to them, if sometimes irritable and impatient. Almost without exception they, and also his male research assistants and Private Secretaries, grew to love him – 'His secretaries adored him . . . We were all in love with him; he was such a lovely man,' said Maurice Ashley, one of his research assistants.

✳

In 1906, confronted by a banner-bearing woman calling for 'Votes for Women', Churchill announced that with such constant disturbance he would not give any such undertaking. 'Nothing would induce me to vote for giving women the franchise. I am not going to be henpecked into a question of such importance,' he is supposed to have declared.

A couple of years later, when his engagement to Clementine Hozier was announced, he was no doubt highly amused to receive a punctuationless telegram reading: 'Hearty congratulations on engagement have great hopes of your speedy conversion but you said you would not be henpecked A Manchester suffragette.'(It is sometimes said that this was Emmeline Pankhurst.)

'At Blenheim I took two very important decisions: to be born and to marry. I am content with the decision I took on both occasions.' Blenheim Palace is the home of the Dukes of Marlborough , cousins of WSC, and was named after the Bavarian village of Blenheim in which the first Duke, John Churchill, and his Austrian allies, defeated the French and Bavarians at the Battle of Blenheim in 1704, during the War of the Spanish Succession.

✳

'I married and lived happily ever after' was how Churchill ended his memoir, *My Early Life.* Balfour once remarked to Churchill upon 'the exaggerated way you tell the truth', which is an excellent description of Churchill's statement.

He certainly could not have been an easy person to live with, given his energy and the strength of his emotions, and the fact that his wife had to share him with the public. Like all marriages theirs had its ups and downs, but it was an affectionate one. Clementine called Winston 'Pig' and he called her 'Cat', or 'Kat', and in the many letters they wrote to each other they called themselves by these nicknames. (There is even a story – surely apocryphal – that some time during Churchill's first premiership, the Archbishop of Canterbury called upon him unexpectedly and was more than a little startled as he walked into the room to find Mr and Mrs Churchill both on all fours on the floor, saying 'oink,

oink' and 'meow' to each other.) That the affection endured is clear in that both the rows and the drollery also endured. Anthony Montague Browne tells of an occasion when, after a row, Clementine swept out of the room saying softly, 'Winston, I have been married to you for forty-five years for better – ' then, loudly '– AND FOR WORSE!' Churchill looked at Montague Browne 'silently for a moment and then observed solemnly: "I am the most unhappy of men." This was so manifestly absurd,' continues Montague Browne, 'that I could not help bursting into an unseemly peal of laughter, which WSC did not seem to mind.'

❈

'It's an extraordinary business, this way of bringing babies into the world. I don't know how God thought if it.'

❈

'My wife and I tried two or three times in the last few years to have breakfast together but it was so disagreeable we had to stop.' Could this be because Clementine liked to get up for breakfast, while her husband's view was that 'Breakfast should be in bed alone'?

In 1918 his mother, aged sixty-four, married a forty-one-year-old archaeologist in the Northern Nigeria Civil Service called Montagu Porch. 'Winston says,' remarked Colonel Repington, *Times* correspondent in the First World War, 'that he hopes marriage won't become the vogue among women his mother's age.' (This was her third marriage and the second time, following WSC's father's death, that she was marrying a man some twenty years her junior.)

✳

Again typical of his time, and also typical of his type, Winston Churchill could treat women with a somewhat heavy-handed half-gallant humour, which would today receive short shrift as bordering on sexual harassment – if the following three stories are to be believed. Strangely, all these examples have something to do with Richmond, Virginia, which seems to abound with large ladies.

At a reception in Richmond, Virginia, in the USA, his hostess, an ample lady, led WSC, the guest of honour, to the buffet table. When she offered him some cold chicken, he asked if he could have a breast. As she helped him to a particularly succulent-looking piece his hostess informed him genteelly that 'We Southern ladies use the term "white meat".'

The next day a corsage arrived for her – with the flowers was a card from Churchill on which he had written 'I would be most obliged if you would pin this on your "white meat".'

✳

While in Washington during a speaking tour of the States, in 1900, Churchill was introduced to a generously proportioned woman – from Richmond, Virginia. Proud of her family's adherence to the former Confederacy, and still not accepting the Reconstruction – the process of incorporating the Southern states into the United States – she declared, as she gave him her hand, 'Mr Churchill, you see before you a rebel who has not been Reconstructed.'

'Madam,' he replied, gazing upon her imposing bosom, 'reconstruction in your case would be blasphemous.'

✳

Getting on for half a century later, Churchill visited Richmond, Virginia, where a sculpture of him was being unveiled. A magnificently Rubenesque lady came up to him and cooed enthusiastically at him: 'Mr Churchill, I want you to know I got up at dawn and drove a hundred miles for the unveiling of your bust.'

Looking upon her generous endowments, WSC answered, 'Madam, I want you to know that I would happily reciprocate the honour.'

Another transatlantic tale, this time from Canada where Churchill was on a speaking tour. At a reception he happened to be seated next to a very strait-laced Methodist minister, when a pert young waitress came up to them with a tray of glasses of sherry. She went first to Churchill, who took a glass, and then turned to the minister. He was appalled to be offered alcohol: 'Young lady,' he announced, 'I'd rather commit adultery than take an intoxicating beverage.' Whereupon Churchill beckoned the girl: 'Come back, miss – I didn't know we had a choice.'

✳

Famously, one of his sparring partners in the House of Commons, and out of it, was Nancy Astor (funnily enough, born in Virginia), of whom he wrote in *Great Contemporaries*: 'She enjoys the best of both worlds . . . she denounces the vice of gambling in unmeasured terms, and is closely associated with an almost unrivalled racing stable. She accepts Communist hospitality and flattery, and remains the Conservative Member for Plymouth.'

✳

The first woman MP to take her seat in Parliament (which she retained from 1919 to 1945), Nancy Astor was among other things a champion of temperance (which Churchill is well known not to have been). On one occasion WSC had just stood up to address the House and was raising a glass of water to his lips when he caught sight of her. 'It must be a great pleasure for the noble lady,' he boomed, 'the member for the Sutton Division of Plymouth, to see me drink water.'

✳

Referring to her taking up her seat in the House of Commons, Churchill remarked (admitting to the sense of discomfiture he had felt at the time), 'Nancy, when you entered the House, I felt you had come upon me in my bath and I had nothing to protect me but my sponge.'

✳

During a debate in the House of Commons, WSC lost patience with Nancy Astor and interrupted her, telling her she was an undesirable alien who should go back home. Lady Astor gave as good as she got, answering 'As for my Right Honourable Friend, he himself is *half* alien and *wholly* undesirable.'

✳

When he eventually came round to the idea of women holding executive positions, he signed the order for their appointment with a flourish and declaration: 'Let there be women!'

The following exchange some claim to be apocryphal, while others suggest that the man in question was not Churchill but someone else – possibly F. E. Smith (Lord Birkenhead); however, there is support – from the Duchess of Marlborough herself – for the argument that it was Churchill. It is said to have taken place at Blenheim when the Astors and the Churchills were guests of the Duke of Marlborough over a weekend, during which Churchill and Nancy Astor apparently argued ferociously the whole time.

Nancy Astor: 'If I were your wife I would put poison in your coffee.'

Churchill: 'Nancy, if I were your husband, I would drink it.'

✳

Newly elected to the House of Commons in 1900, the young Churchill thought that a moustache might add dignity and maturity to his youthful looks. Not long after a woman came up to him, and said forthrightly: 'There are two things I don't like about you, Mr Churchill – your politics and your moustache.' Already then, it would seem, he was never at a loss for the satisfying retort: 'My dear madam,' he replied, 'pray do not disturb yourself. You are not likely to come into contact with either,'

Leaving the Commons bar one evening, it is said, Churchill ran into another woman MP, the formidable Bessie Braddock. 'Winston,' she said icily, 'you're drunk.' Churchill drew himself up: 'Madam, you're ugly. But tomorrow I shall be shober.'

✳

'It is hard, if not impossible, to snub a beautiful woman – they remain beautiful and the rebuke recoils.'

✳

The question 'If you could not be who you are, who would you like to be?' was making the round of the dinner table; eventually it was Churchill's turn, and everybody waited expectantly to hear what the great former wartime prime minister would say. 'If I could not be who I am, I would most like to be . . .' he paused for effect, then, turning to Clementine: 'Mrs Churchill's second husband.'

✳

'My most brilliant achievement was to persuade my wife to marry me.'

Churchill's second daughter Sarah was first married – not for very long – to an American-Austrian popular comedian called Vic Oliver. Over twenty years older than her and twice divorced, he was not considered at all suitable and the Churchills did what they could to stop the marriage, but it went ahead anyway, and they became more or less reconciled to it – though they did consider Oliver 'common'. It is said that at dinner one evening, Oliver, who had brought along a guest, wanted to draw out his famous father-in-law. 'Who,' he asked, 'in your opinion, is the greatest statesman you know?'

That was a mistake. Churchill emerged from his gloomy reverie and answered smartly and unexpectedly: 'Benito Mussolini.'

'What? Why?'

'Mussolini is the only statesman who had the requisite courage to have his son-in-law executed.'

(Mussolini's son-in-law was his Foreign Minister, Count Ciano.)

✳

When, in 1960, a reporter from the London *Evening Standard* asked Churchill what he thought about the recent prediction that by the year 2000 women would be ruling the world, he muttered gloomily in reply, 'They still will, will they?'

One day in 1953, five-year-old Nicholas Soames, son of Churchill's daughter Mary Soames, was on a visit to Chartwell. Hearing the way the grown-ups were talking about WSC, he understood just one thing of what they were saying and hastened out of the room to have it confirmed by the horse's mouth, running upstairs. 'Grandpapa!' he cried, bursting into the Prime Minister's bedroom, where he was in bed working on a speech. 'Grandpapa, are you really the greatest man in the world?'

'Of course I am the greatest man in the world,' growled Churchill. 'Now bu– buzz off.'

✻

Discussing with his friend, the poet Wilfred Scawen Blunt the violent action of some suffragettes he had recently encountered, Churchill did not fail to appropriate the following comment on what he saw as the absurdity of their habit of chaining themselves to railings: 'I might as well chain myself to St Thomas's [Hospital] and say I would not move until I had had a baby!'

'An ineradicable habit':
Drink

Whether or not Churchill had a 'drink problem' seems to have been for long a favourite topic for discussion. That he enjoyed alcohol – especially whisky, brandy and champagne – is beyond doubt, but that he was a drunkard seems quite unlikely. His slight speech impediment, slurring S's into Shs and Zhs, might have suggested to those who did not know any better the speech of a drinker – and it could well have suited Churchill from time to time to give the impression that he was the worse for drink, that his brain was perhaps not working as acutely as it actually was . . . In general, the alcohol issue fed his sense of mischief: while he had a proper respect for fine brandies or champagnes, it amused him to talk about his drinking habits, and to tease teetotallers. (And apparently after Churchill's car accident in January 1932 in New York, Dr Otto C. Pickhardt wrote a prescription for him . . . 'the use of alcoholic spirits at meal times . . . the minimum requirement to be 250 cc'.) Drunkenness, on the other hand, was not on: 'I have been brought up and trained to have the utmost contempt for people who get drunk,' he wrote in *My Early Life*.

✳

Churchill's reply to Field Marshal Montgomery's smug statement, 'I neither drink nor smoke and am a hundred per cent fit,' was inevitable: '*I* drink and smoke and I am *two* hundred per cent fit.'

'When I was a young subaltern in the South
African War, the water was not fit to drink. To make
it palatable we had to add whisky. By diligent effort
I learned to like it,' he said, according to Anthony
Montague Browne, his last Private Secretary.

✳

'I neither want it [brandy] nor need it, but I should
think it pretty hazardous to interfere with the
ineradicable habit of a lifetime.'

✳

'No one can say that I ever failed to display a meet
and proper appreciation of alcohol.'

✳

A letter to his wife Clementine in 1924 when he'd
just moved, ahead of her, into the newly acquired
Chartwell suggests that wine played an important
part in his daily life; he clearly wants to assure
Clementine that he is suffering no great hardship
(though what he means by 'buckets' is debatable): 'I
drink champagne at all meals & buckets of claret &
soda in between . . .'

In 1939, however, when *Picture Post* decided to support a campaign in favour of Churchill's return to office, the magazine's picture editor related, when the camera was set up Churchill put the brandy glasses under the table and covered them up with a napkin in case readers got the wrong impression.

✳

On hearing, during a lunch with the King of Saudi Arabia, Ibn Saud, that the king's religion forbade drinking and smoking, Churchill couldn't resist announcing (though presumably not to Ibn Saud's face): 'I must point out that my rule of life prescribes as an absolutely sacred rite smoking cigars and also the drinking of alcohol before, after, and if need be during all meals and in the intervals between them.'

✳

'Always remember, Clemmie, that I have taken more out of alcohol than alcohol has taken out of me.'

✳

'Good cognac is like a woman. Do not assault it. Coddle and warm it in your hands before you sip it.'

'When I was younger I made it a rule never to take strong drink before lunch. It is now my rule never to do so before breakfast.'

✳

It is related that when Churchill was First Lord of the Admiralty, he was approached by a temperance group suggesting that he should reconsider the maritime tradition of christening a ship by breaking a bottle of champagne across the bow (they felt that the practice added an undesirable glamour to champagne).

'But, madam,' Churchill replied to the group's spokeswoman, 'the hallowed custom of the Royal Navy is indeed a splendid example of temperance. The ship takes its first sip of wine and then proceeds on water ever after.'

✳

The diplomat Lord Harvey remarked in 1942 of Churchill's desire to fly to India '. . . how gallant of the old boy himself! But his age and more especially his way of life must begin to tell on him. He had beer, three ports and three brandies for lunch today, and has done it for years.'

According to Major-General Ian Jacob of Churchill's wartime Defence Staff (later Sir Ian Jacob, Governor of the BBC), however, 'He always had a bottle of champagne for lunch.' John Peck, one of Churchill's Private Secretaries, pointed out that Ian Jacob had rarely had lunch with Churchill, and that in any case the PM only ever have had a glass or two – that the rest of the bottle would go elsewhere. John Peck also declared firmly, ' I *never* saw him the worse for drink. The glass of weak whisky, like the cigars, was more a symbol than anything else, and one glass lasted for hours.'

※

Certainly the view Churchill expresses here seems that of a connoisseur, not that of a mere boozer: 'A single glass of champagne imparts a feeling of exhilaration. The nerves are braced, the imagination is agreeably stirred, the wits become more nimble. A bottle produces the contrary effect.'

Lord Hailes who, as Patrick Buchan-Hepburn, had also been a Private Secretary to WSC, corroborated this: 'I never knew him to get drunk. He sipped coloured water all day, from morning to night: there was hardly any whisky in it at all.' While yet another Private Secretary, the diplomat and writer Sir David Hunt, said, ' He certainly drank the weakest whisky-and-soda that I have ever known.'

Having a bottle always on the table had other uses, in any case. One of Churchill's frequent visitors in the years before the war was Major Desmond Morton, a former member of the government's secret Industrial Intelligence Centre. When, after the war, Jock Colville asked Churchill outright if Morton had been giving him – when he was 'in the wilderness' – more information than the government would have approved, Churchill's answer was, 'Have another drop of brandy.'

✻

As a pleasing footnote, a token of champagne's appreciation of Churchill:

When many of the trees at Chartwell were lost in the 1987 'hurricane' a large number of them were replaced by the Pol Roger family. It is said, too, that during the Second World War, Madame Pol Roger had two cases of champagne for Churchill, which she kept hidden from the Nazis. Needless to say, Pol Roger champagne was Churchill's favourite.

'Gleaming toys':
Anecdotes

'Anecdotes,' Churchill once remarked, 'are the gleaming toys of House of Commons history.' Unsurprisingly, there are a great many such 'gleaming toys' about him. In the selection that follows some of the stories are definitely authentic, but there are no doubt many that have been embellished; or have changed in details such as date, location, even characters, as they have been told and retold. But if the details are not always in accordance with other versions of the story, they have been selected for their Churchillian flavour.

✳

A famous early indication of Churchill's defiant nature occurred at Harrow when, aged thirteen or so, he was summoned before the headmaster over some matter of ill-discipline or idleness. 'I have very grave reason to be displeased with you,' intoned the good Mr Welldon (for whom Churchill long retained an affection). 'And I, sir, have very grave reason to be displeased with you,' rejoined the boy.

On another occasion at school, Churchill was asked by his Latin teacher to decline *mensa* (table). The boy proceeded to do so, giving the nominative, accusative, genitive, dative and ablative. 'The vocative?' prompted his teacher.

'But I don't intend ever to talk to tables,' Churchill replied reasonably, if impertinently.

A few years before the outbreak of the First World War, Churchill was at a diplomatic reception. An Italian military attaché asked a Luxembourgeois diplomat about a medal he was wearing. 'It is an ancient order called the Royal Admiralty Cross,' the diplomat replied stiffly. After he had stalked off, the Italian turned to the First Lord of the Admiralty, Winston Churchill, and remarked how odd it was that Luxembourg should have this when it did not even have a navy. 'Why shouldn't they have an admiralty?' Churchill answered cheerfully. 'You in Italy, after all, have a minister of finance – yet you don't have a treasury!'

✳

Travelling across the United States in 1929, with his son Randolph, brother Jack and Jack's boy, Johnny, Churchill's itinerary took in Hollywood, where he met Charlie Chaplin. In conversation with him, Churchill asked what film part he would like to do next. In all seriousness, Chaplin replied, 'I'd like to play Jesus Christ.'

Without batting an eyelid, WSC asked him: 'Have you cleared the rights?'

There is a tale that, following the British withdrawal in 1940 from Norway, it was proposed that the Royal Marines should all have sheaths to protect the exposed muzzles of their rifles from the sharp temperature changes for their next foray into Norway. A pharmaceutical company that specialized in manufacturing condoms was given the job. In due course the first box was delivered for the Prime Minister's inspection. He looked at the box and muttered, 'Won't do.' He drew a carton out of the box, shook his head and muttered 'Won't do' again. He opened the carton and took out a packet. 'Won't do,' he reiterated.

'What do you mean it won't do?' an aide asked him. 'They are long enough for the muzzles – ten and a half inches.'

'Labels,' came the cryptic reply.

'*Labels?*'

'Yes. I want a label for every box, every carton, every packet, saying "British. Size: Medium". That will show the Nazis, if they ever recover one of them, who's the master race.'

✳

Another story has it that while visiting a parachute factory, Churchill absentmindedly took out a cigar. Immediately, the fire officer came running up: 'Sir, sir, you mustn't smoke!' he cried out.

'Oh, don't worry, dear boy,' came the reply. 'I don't inhale.'

According to legend, during the late 1920s or early 1930s, at a time when Churchill was speaking out against those who argued that the League of Nations and the power of civilized negotiation would secure peace, and calling for greater expenditure on defence, he addressed the St George Society. His theme was how a contemporary St George would save a maiden from the dragon.

'St George would be accompanied, not by a horse, but by a delegation. He would be armed not with a lance, but by a secretariat . . . he would propose a conference with the dragon – a Round Table conference – no doubt that would be more convenient for the dragon's tail.

'Then after making a trade agreement with the dragon, St George would lend the dragon a lot of money.' He continued in this vein for a bit, until 'The maiden's release would be referred to the League of Nations of Geneva, and finally St George would be photographed with the dragon.'

✳

Securing the wholehearted compliance of the Free French during the war was not always easy, especially when it required the co-operation of both de Gaulle and the Vichy French. Urged by a diplomat to coddle de Gaulle's pride with flattery, Churchill is said to have to have agreed: 'I'll kiss him on both cheeks – or, if you prefer, on all four.'

To an admiral who had protested that Churchill's suggested provision of better conditions for ordinary seamen was 'against the traditions' of the Royal Navy, Churchill is said to have retorted: 'Traditions! What traditions? Rum, sodomy – and the lash!' Anthony Montague Brown said of the phrase that Churchill 'liked it very much, but he had never heard it before'. Another of his Private Secretaries, Jock Colville, on the other hand, seems to think that Churchill did utter those words – to Sir Dudley Pound, adding that 'Pound had a slow, wry sense of humour, but this was going too far.'

On another occasion, Churchill was heard to remark of Pound, 'Dudley Pound's a funny old boy. People think he's always asleep, but you've only got to suggest reducing the naval estimates by a million and he's awake in a flash.'

✳

In the early days of the Blitz, Churchill was driven to Canterbury where he went to view the cathedral being bolstered with sandbags. The Archbishop was gloomy, and the Prime Minister attempted to bolster him up too: 'No matter how many close hits the Nazis may make, I feel sure the cathedral will survive.' 'Ah, *close* hits . . .,' said the Archbishop glumly. 'But what if we get a *direct* hit?'

'In that event,' the Prime Minister responded, losing patience, 'you will have to regard it, my dear Archbishop, as a divine summons.'

When in Casablanca to meet President Roosevelt in 1943, WSC expressed an interest in strolling through the Kasbah. This caused alarm among his security guards who could not guarantee his safety in such a place. Knowing, however, that Churchill would not be swayed by considerations of his personal safety, they earnestly pointed out to him that the Kasbah was an unhealthy place where he might contract some terrible oriental infection – which he might even pass on to the President of the United States. Wickedly, the Prime Minister chose to play along with them but also to carry matters a bit further. . . 'Ah ha! So you think there's life in the old dog yet, do you? I assure you, my friends, that even if I were to go to the Kasbah and contract the disease which you have in mind, I should be most unlikely to communicate it to the President.'

*

During the early years of the Second World War the First Sea Lord was Admiral Sir Dudley Pound, elderly, earnest, conscientious, slow, but an object of the Prime Minister's affection and esteem. One summer night after dinner at Chequers they were walking in the rose-garden when the Admiral – indisputably sober, but lame – slipped on some steps and fell flat on his back. Gazing down on him, Churchill admonished the poor man fondly: 'Try to remember that you are an Admiral of the Fleet and not a midshipman.'

During his wartime premiership especially, Churchill was careful to study all the letters, papers and articles that had been considered worth his perusal by his ministers and other officials. Those that he wished to follow up were passed on to his Private Secretaries for action. On one occasion these included a Washington press summary on which the Prime Minister had scrawled 'Who is the author of these brilliant if somewhat perfervid reports?' One of the Private Secretaries, Jock Colville, made enquiries and then returned the paper with the note: 'The author is Isaiah Berlin.'

Nothing more was said and time passed. Then, early in February 1944, the Churchills gave a luncheon party at 10 Downing Street. Just before, Mrs Churchill mentioned to Colville, in some puzzlement, that the her husband had insisted on her inviting, at short notice, Irving Berlin, the popular American songwriter and composer of musicals, whose arrival in London to entertain the troops had been widely publicized.

Mr Berlin duly arrived and was introduced. He kept discreetly quiet during the excellent lunch. Then, at the end of lunch, the Prime Minister turned to him and asked, 'Now, Mr Berlin, tell us what in your opinion is the likelihood of my dear friend, the President, being re-elected for a fourth term.' Mr Berlin, overcome, gabbled about how he was honoured and flattered . . . 'Gee, to think that Winston Churchill should ask me, Irving Berlin, a question of that importance on which I am so little qualified to speak.'

'Come, Mr Berlin. As the author of those brilliant if somewhat perfervid reports, your impressions will be of great interest.' As Irving Berlin launched into a rambling explanation of why he thought Roosevelt would be re-elected, Colville suddenly twigged. Fearing that this was leading to utter embarrassment all round, he kicked Churchill under the table.

'What are you kicking me for?' the Prime Minister boomed plaintively. As Colville muttered some lame excuse one of the other guests realized that something was not quite as it should be and deftly steered the conversation away from the presidential election.

(The story eventually reached the ears of Isaiah Berlin, the historian, philosopher and writer, who was ecstatic.)

✳

Shortly after returning from a tour of the Near East in 1940, Anthony Eden presented to the Prime Minister a report on his findings of such long-windedness that Churchill reportedly returned it to his War Minister with a note reading: 'As far as I can see you have used every cliché except "Prepare to meet thy God" and "Please adjust your dress before leaving".' (Churchill denied this story, but it has an undeniably Churchillian ring. Anthony Eden was, incidentally, Jack Churchill's son-in-law.)

As Minister of Fuel and Power in 1947, Hugh Gaitskell, later Attlee's successor as leader of the Labour Party, had advocated saving energy by taking fewer baths: 'Personally, I have never had a great many baths myself, and I can assure those who are in the habit of having a great many that it does not make a great difference to their health if they have less.' Churchill, famous for having baths, responded: 'When Ministers of the Crown speak like this on behalf of His Majesty's Government, the Prime Minister and his friends have no need to wonder why they are getting increasingly into bad odour. I have even asked myself, when meditating upon these points, whether you, Mr Speaker, would admit the word "lousy" as a Parliamentary expression in referring to the Administration, provided, of course, it was not intended in a contemptuous sense but purely as one of factual narration.'

✳

When staying at the White House as a guest of President Roosevelt, Churchill naturally had a bathroom to himself and could have a bath whenever he wished. Roosevelt's son recalled his father trundling into Churchill's room in his wheelchair to see his guest, and being startled to catch a naked Churchill just stepping out of his bath. He hurriedly set about reversing his wheelchair but was stopped by Churchill: 'The Prime Minister has nothing to hide from the President of the United States.'

Churchill was *apparently* none too good at speaking foreign languages, and certainly seemed to refuse stubbornly to try to pronounce words correctly (especially names – he himself said, 'Everybody has a right to pronounce foreign names as he chooses'). Jock Colville recalled an instance in 1941 when as Churchill's Private Secretary he was caught uncomfortably between Churchill and de Gaulle. General de Gaulle was at the time being a less than helpful ally and the Prime Minister, considerably annoyed by his behaviour, summoned him to Downing Street. (Perhaps it was this or a similar occasion that inspired Churchill's comment, 'There is only one thing worse than fighting with allies and that is fighting without them.') He informed Jock Colville that he would not shake hands with de Gaulle and would not speak with him in French but through an interpreter – and that Colville himself was to be the interpreter.

The General arrived at the due time and was ushered into the Cabinet Room. True to his word, Churchill did not shake his hand, merely indicating a seat across the table from himself. 'General de Gaulle, I have asked you to come here this afternoon,' he started and looked fiercely at Colville, who translated: 'Mon Général, je vous ai invité . . .'

'I *didn't* say "Mon Général",' objected Churchill petulantly, 'and I did not say I had *invited* him.'

Colville struggled on for a few sentences, with many interruptions from his boss. Then de Gaulle spoke and Colville interpreted – to be interrupted by, 'Non, non. Ce n'est pas du tout le sens de ce que je disais.' At which Churchill said that if he could not do any better he had better find someone who could. A half-ashamed, half-relieved Colville escaped and summoned someone from the Foreign Office whose French was impeccable. The official arrived in next to no time and Colville showed him into the Cabinet Room (in which not a word had been spoken during the interval).

Within minutes the man from the Foreign Office came out red-faced, and spluttering that they had to be mad: they had said he could not speak French properly and they would have to manage without an interpreter.

The soundproof double doors of the Cabinet Room were closed and nothing could be heard. Over an hour passed and Colville was beginning to get anxious – 'Perhaps they had strangled each other?' But then the bell rang and he went in – to find the two men sitting amicably side by side, smoking cigars and chatting – in French.

✳

The Queen Mother told Colville a rather curious tale about Churchill's visiting Buckingham Palace shortly after the Partition of India, which established Pakistan as an autonomous nation. He stood in the doorway of the drawing-room where the King and Queen (as the Queen Mother was then) were waiting for him, bowed and said, 'I believe that this is the first time I have had the honour to be invited to luncheon by the King and Queen of Pakistan.'

✳

At a reception the actor Sir Cedric Hardwicke was introduced to Churchill. 'I am honoured to learn that I am your favourite British actor,' he gushed. WSC did not like gushing. 'Yesh,' he growled. 'And my fifth favourite actor: the first four are the Marx Brothers.'

✳

By 1953, Churchill was becoming somewhat deaf. The Italian government, as is still its wont, had just fallen, and the ousted Italian premier, a friend of WSC's told him, was planning to retire and read the works of Anthony Trollope.

There was a long silence. Then: 'Tell me more about that trollop,' said Churchill.

A few years later, an MP called Bernard Braine was speaking during a debate in the House of Commons. WSC couldn't see him and asked his neighbour, Julian Amery, a Conservative MP and son of WSC's old friend Leo Amery, who it was speaking. 'Braine,' answered Amery. 'James?' 'No, *Braine*.' 'Drain?' said Churchill. 'He can't be called Drain. Nobody's called Drain.'

Finding a scrap of paper, Julian Amery wrote the name down. 'Ah, I see,' Churchill said. '. . . Is he well named?'

Child-like, Churchill believed that wherever he was his domestic routine would be the same as at home. One day, when the Supreme War Council were meeting at the Château du Muguet in June 1940 – just after Dunkirk, with the fall of France imminent – General Spears reported, two French officers, drinking coffee in the dining room, were alarmed by the doors being flung open and 'an apparition which they said resembled an angry Japanese genie, in long, flowing red silk kimono over other similar but white garments, girdled with a white belt' burst in, 'sparse hair on end' and loudly demanded, 'Oo ay ma ban?'

✳

It is said that on one occasion during the war Churchill, due to deliver an address to the nation at eight p.m., for some reason had to take a taxi to the BBC studio. As one drew up, WSC's aide told the driver the destination. 'Sorry, guv, can't take you there, I've got to get home quick to listen to the Prime Minister's speech on me radio.'

This, of course, greatly pleased Churchill, who handed a five-pound note to his aide to pass on to the cabbie, saying, 'I'm in a hurry to get to that address.'

Delighted with the five pounds (a lot of money in those days), and hopeful of more to come, the cabbie quickly opened the passenger doors: 'Get in, guv'nor. Frig the bloody Prime Minister – what's that address again?'

The late Sir Robert Rhodes James, for many years a Tory MP and, among much else, the editor of Churchill's speeches, liked to tell two stories about WSC.

One evening during the war, probably in 1942, Churchill was dining in the underground dining room of the Cabinet War Rooms. With him (we have to assume) were General Sir Alan Brooke, as well as the PM's secretary, possibly his daughter Mary, and one or two others. As the meal began, WSC seemed in good form, chatting and joking with his companions. At that point down the stairs came, rather late, Admiral Lord Louis ('Dickie') Mountbatten (later Admiral of the Fleet Earl Mountbatten of Burma), at that time Chief of Combined Operations, and an important figure in that Combined Ops was responsible for amphibious operations against German forces in Occupied Europe. Mountbatten was as usual gorgeously turned out in a tailored admiral's uniform, gold braid, medal ribbons, and all the other trappings of high rank, and immediately began to exercise his considerable charm upon the gathering, talking to everyone, rehearsing interesting aspects of policy, retailing snippets of gossip. He shone, in short (the word Robert used of his conversation was 'coruscating'). Everyone responded to his warmth and wit – except WSC, who became more and more silent, refusing food, sitting slumped in his chair with a cigar and a glass of brandy, saying nothing and occasionally glowering at the late arrival.

Mountbatten took no notice, but eventually rose, threw down his napkin, announced that he had yet more important meetings to attend that night, summoned his Wren driver, bid a gracious goodnight to all, and made a dashing exit. As he neared the top of the stairs, and while he was still just in earshot, WSC looked up and finally broke his silence: 'Do I know that young man?' he remarked loudly. Thereafter a rejuvenated Churchill once more joined the party, and became the life and soul of the evening.

(It was WSC who appointed Mountbatten to his post as Chief of Combined Operations – and remarked of him 'He is a triphibian – equally at home on land, sea or air; and he has experienced a bit of fire too.')

✻

Some years later – presumably after 1955, when he ceded the premiership to Eden – Churchill was sitting in an armchair in the Members' Bar of the House of Commons. He was alone. Three young Tory MPs entered and, failing to see the old boy slouched in his armchair, began to chatter loudly. It soon became clear that the Member for Epping was the subject of their talk.

'You know,' one remarked, 'it's very sad about old Winston. He's getting awfully forgetful.'

'Shame, isn't it?' said another. 'He's really very doddery now, I gather.'

'Not only that,' added the third, 'but I've heard that he's going a bit – *you* know – *ga-ga*.'

'Yesh,' rumbled a deep voice from the nearby armchair, 'an' they shay he'sh gettin' terribly deaf, as well!'

✳

Sitting in the House of Commons in 1956, listening to Hugh Gaitskell speaking on economic issues, Churchill suddenly began rummaging through his pockets, and then bending down to search the floor and under his seat. Gaitskell, completely thrown off-track, stopped speaking and asked if he could help. 'I was only looking for my jujube,' WSC answered in a small voice, loud enough to be heard by the whole House. (The following day the newspapers wrote this up under the heading 'the Fall of the Pastille'.)

✳

Churchill didn't tolerate fools much – or, indeed, at all – but at various times during the war was saddled with aides, usually young, who were not always as quick-witted or perceptive as they might have been. One day one of these aides, a junior officer, found Churchill reading the paper at breakfast, looking decidedly down in the mouth.

'I say, sir,' remarked the young man, 'you look rather glum.'

'I am. I've just read here' – jabbing the paper – 'that the Duke of Wellin'ton's son has been killed.'

'Oh, rotten luck! You mean the young duke, sir?'

'No! I mean the hero of the Peninshula!'

(Apart from Waterloo, the first Duke of Wellington's greatest victories were over the French in the Peninsular War of 1808–14.)

✳

On another occasion the PM was in the garden at 10 Downing Street, taking a stroll on a fine summer's evening in the company of another young aide (or perhaps even the same one).

Spotting something among the flowers and shrubs, the young man cried, 'I say, sir, look at this!' and rushed towards whatever it was, only to trip over his own feet and fall head first into a rosebush.(Prime ministerial rose gardens seem to have attracted tumbles.)

WSC sighed, looked up at the sky and said loudly, 'O Lord, the foolzh Thou shendesht me to win thish war!'

In the Great Hall of Chequers is a large Rubens painting of the Aesop fable in which a lion caught in a net is rescued by a mouse nibbling at the rope binding the net to a tree. According to Harold Wilson, Churchill decided late one night: 'Can't see the moushe', and called for his paints and brushes. He then set about painting in the mouse.

Whatever the truth, some time later the painting was lent to a fund-raising exhibition for Churchill College, Cambridge, and was cleaned – if mouse there had been, it came off.

✳

Churchill did not like Aneurin Bevan – not because of his politics; WSC had the wisdom not to let such matters interfere with friendships – and the sentiment was reciprocated. In parliamentary debates between them, Churchill usually came out on top – even if only because he could make the House laugh. One day they had a rather different confrontation. In June 1953, on the occasion of Elizabeth II's coronation, Lancaster House, newly refurbished, was the location for the Foreign Secretary's Coronation Banquet at which Churchill acted as host since Anthony Eden was ill. The guests included the entire royal family and the representatives of many foreign countries, all magnificently dressed.

After the banquet, they all repaired to Buckingham Palace where there was a State Ball.

The company presented a stunning spectacle, the military and naval in full dress uniform, others decked out in fine court dress, or at the very least white tie and tails, many garlanded with decorations.

On arriving at Buckingham Palace, Churchill quickly nipped into a lavatory. When he emerged through the fine mahogany door he came face to face with Bevan – wearing a blue serge suit. 'I think,' admonished the Prime Minister, 'that at least on this occasion you might have taken the trouble to dress properly.'

Bevan gave a crocodile smile: 'Prime Minister, your fly buttons are undone.'

(Churchill might have pointed out, echoing another exchange, that in a couple of minutes his fly buttons would be done up, but Bevan would still be unsuitably dressed.)

✳

Fly buttons feature in another story about Churchill – it is said that on one occasion, when advised that his fly buttons were undone, he replied, 'Dead birds don't fall out of their nests.'

Surveying the destroyers sent to Britain by the USA under the Lend-Lease Agreement set up in 1940, Churchill gazed at the barely seaworthy vessels and mumbled to himself gloomily, 'Cheap and nasty.' 'Pardon me?' asked Roosevelt's envoy, standing next to him. Quick-thinking, the Prime Minister amended his remark: 'Cheap for us, and nasty for the Germans.'

It is possible that the envoy was Harry Hopkins, special adviser to Roosevelt and administrator of the Lend-Lease programme, a man as unlike Churchill himself as was possible – and with whom he struck up an instant friendship. In autumn 1941 Churchill travelled by destroyer with Hopkins to Newfoundland to have a meeting with President Roosevelt. At dinner the first evening, WSC opened a pot of caviar, a present from Stalin, saying, 'Ah, Mr Hopkins, it is good to have such a treat, even if it means fighting on the side of the Russians to get it.'

On that same trip, Churchill had enough time to himself to read a book for pleasure – this was *Captain Hornblower, RN*, which had been sent by a friend. He greatly enjoyed C. S. Forester's novel, and when security permitted he sent a signal to his friend, at the time at GHQ in Egypt: 'Hornblower admirable.' This caused great consternation and confusion at GHQ – clearly a codeword, they told themselves, but why did nobody have a clue as to what it might mean?

One evening in the 1950s, Churchill was spending a quiet evening with a group of close friends. One of them remarked upon how ironical it was that the countries that had lost the war – Germany and Japan – were now the most prosperous in the world, while the victors, Britain and the United States, seemed to be in an increasingly poor economic state.

'Well,' suggested another light-heartedly, 'we might fight another war and lose it?' After a few moments' silence, Churchill rumbled into life. 'Um,' he said. 'And whom do you propose we should fight it againsht?'

'I thought that we might declare war on the United States . . .' came the mischievous reply.

A few more moments' silence before the rumble: 'Um, well . . . Yesh, but, you shee, we wouldn't lozhe.'

✳

On Churchill's eightieth birthday, in 1964, a young man was sent to take his photograph. Full of awe, he breathed, 'Sir Winston, it is wonderful to take your photograph on your eightieth birthday and I do look forward to taking it again on your hundredth birthday.' Kindly, the great man replied, 'Young man, you appear to me to be in good health and sound in wind and limb. So I see no reason why you should not.'

Referring to Churchill's 'puckish approach to solemn occasions', Anthony Montague Browne described an instance when the Crown Prince of Japan was lunching at Number 10 during Churchill's second premiership, when relations between Japan and Britain were doubtless somewhat stiff and formal. In a bid for diversion, Churchill sent for two fifteenth-century Japanese bronzes that his mother had brought back from the Far East. They were of a stallion, gazing at a mare in season. Passing them to the Crown Prince he remarked that these epitomized to him 'sex in bronze'. The Crown Prince turned them over and over, inspecting them closely. 'You won't find it there,' muttered Churchill.

✳

There is a story that on a parliamentary paper that was being circulated, someone scribbled in the margin against a statement with which he disagreed the words 'Round objects!' He was probably congratulating himself on his wit, and thinking how the PM would appreciate his droll comment, when the paper made its way back to him – beside his words was scrawled in Churchill's handwriting: 'Who is Round? And why does he object?'

Anthony Montague Browne in his account of his years as Churchill's Private Secretary wrote of how much Churchill disliked being interrupted while he was at work. On one occasion in the 1950s, as he worked on a speech in bed, the Foreign Secretary and the Chancellor of the Exchequer (Eden and Butler) arrived to see him urgently. They followed his secretary upstairs and stood outside the bedroom door while Montague Browne went in to announce their visit to the Prime Minister. 'Tell them to go and bugger themselves,' they heard. Then, as Montague Browne was coming out: 'There is no need for them to carry out that instruction literally.'

'Our maxims will remain':
Epigrams

Like all self-respecting wits, Churchill was a fount of epigrams – his own, 'borrowed' ones, and well-known ones that he adapted.

Among his most famous words is the epigraph:

> 'In war: resolution
> In defeat: defiance
> In victory: magnanimity
> In peace: goodwill.'

(It is said to have originally been offered, at the end of the First World War, to a French town as a memorial; the lines, however, were politely declined – apparently on the grounds that the shattered citizens found the idea of magnanimity and goodwill too hard to take. Certainly French 'reparations' against Germany at Versailles bear this out.)

✳

'Too often the strong silent man is silent because he does not know what to say, and is reputed strong only because he has remained silent.'

✳

'It is better to be making the news than taking it; to be an actor rather than a critic.'

'Perhaps it is better to be irresponsible and right than to be responsible and wrong.'

✳

'A fanatic is one who can't change his mind and won't change the subject.'

✳

'It is a fine thing to be honest, but it is also very important to be right.'

✳

'Art is to beauty what honour is to honesty.'

✳

'Without tradition art is a flock of sheep without a shepherd. Without innovation it is a corpse.'

✳

'Youth is for freedom and reform, maturity for judicious compromise, and old age for stability and repose.'

'Civil servants – no longer servants, no longer civil.'

✳

'If the present tries to sit in judgement of the past, it will lose the future.'

✳

'When civilization degenerates our morals will be gone but our maxims will remain.'

✳

'Diplomacy is the art of telling plain truths without giving offence.'

✳

'Everyone has his day and some days last longer than others.'

✳

'Do not let the better be the enemy of the good.' (These words he spoke to one of his literary assistants, John Wheldon, whose concern with finer detail was slowing down his work. Churchill said much the same thing in a different manner on another occasion: 'The maxim "Nothing avails but perfection" may be spelt p-a-r-a-l-y-s-i-s.')

'There are a terrible lot of lies going around the world, and the worst of it is half of them are true.'

✳

'We are happier in many ways when we are old than when we are young. The young sow wild oats, the old grow sage.'

✳

'War is mainly a catalogue of blunders.'

✳

'A nation that forgets its past has no future.'

✳

'Never stand so high upon a principle that you cannot lower it to suit the circumstances.'

✳

'It is always wise to look ahead, but difficult to look farther than you can see'

✳

'You will never get to the end of the journey if you stop to shy a stone at every dog that barks.'

'Virtuous motives, trammelled by inertia and timidity, are no match for armed and resolute wickedness.'

✳

'The worst quarrels only arise when both sides are equally in the right and in the wrong.'

✳

'Criticism is easy; achievement is difficult.'

✳

'It is always more easy to discover and proclaim general principles than to apply them.'

✳

'Never trust a man who has not a single redeeming vice.'

✳

'It is wonderful how well men can keep secrets they have not been told.'

This remark was apropos of his failure, as a war correspondent during the Boer War, to learn of an intended campaign from senior officers.

'Sometimes truth is so precious, it must be attended by a bodyguard of lies.' WSC, speaking at the Tehran Conference in 1943, was referring specifically to Allied plans for the invasion of Europe. (In the event Operation Overlord, the codename for the brilliantly successful Normandy landings in June 1944, was attended, and in many respects made possible, by a series of imaginative and astonishingly effective deception operations – or 'lies'.)

※

'Difficulties mastered are opportunities won.'

Miscellanea

'I decline utterly to be impartial as between the fire brigade and the fire.' (Speaking to the House in July 1926, during the General Strike, Churchill was responding to complaints about bias in his editing of the *British Gazette*.)

✳

'Physician, comb thyself.' (The 'physician' in this speech to the House of Commons in May 1916 was the War Office, which was calling for the 'combing-out', or pruning, of industries and of other government departments.)

✳

'Well, the principle seems the same. The water still keeps falling over.' Churchill was clearly irritated at being asked if the Niagara Falls looked the same as when he first saw them.

✳

'If it is a blessing, it is certainly very well disguised.' It is said that Clementine remarked that his defeat in the 1945 election was perhaps a blessing in disguise; he did not agree.

Even on the most serious of occasions, Churchill could not resist little jokes, and when he arrived on the Normandy beachhead on D-Day-plus-6 (12 June 1944) to meet Montgomery, he sent Roosevelt a postcard: 'Wish you were here.'

✳

'It's a nuizenza to have the fluenza,' Churchill wrote irrefutably to Roosevelt in 1942.

✳

Early in 1945, there was an exchange of letters between President Roosevelt and Churchill about the agenda for the Yalta conference. The American President could not see any reason why they could not complete the plans for establishing the UN during the six days of the conference. Churchill wrote back: 'I don't see any way of realizing our hopes for a World Organization in six days. Even the Almighty took seven.'

✳

On a visit to New York in the early 1930s, Churchill was taken to a game of American football. Asked what he thought of it, he replied, 'Actually it is somewhat like rugby. But why do you have all these committee meetings?'

In May 1955, a BBC spokesman defended an impending programme, a debate entitled *Christianity vs. Atheism*, pointing out 'It is our duty to truth to allow both sides to debate.'

'I suppose, then, that if there had been the same devices at the time of Christ,' Churchill retorted, 'the BBC would have given equal time to Judas and Jesus.'

✳

Seated one day with the dour director-general of the BBC, Lord Reith, a tall Presbyterian Scot of gloomy aspect, Churchill was heard to mutter, 'Who will rescue me from this Wuthering Height?'

✳

Although he played golf – and probably enjoyed it – Churchill was clearly not an obsessive bore about the game: 'Golf is like chasing a quinine pill around a pasture,' he once remarked. And on another occasion: 'Golf is a game whose aim is to hit a very small ball into an even smaller hole, with weapons singularly ill designed for the purpose.'

(A friend of his, Lord Riddell, told of a game of golf they had together in 1911, when they came across an earthworm on the golf course. WSC gently picked up the worm and placed it in the bracken, saying, 'Poor fellow! If I leave you here, you will be trampled upon by some ruthless boot.')

'Surely there never was an army which marched like the army of science.' But, dismayed at the comparative failure of the United Kingdom to produce as many scientists and engineers as the United States, Churchill spoke soon after ending his last term as Prime Minister about how he should have tried to see the establishment in Britain of an equivalent to the Massachusetts Institute of Technology. His former secretary Jock Colville and others immediately set about making amends, raising funds for a new college which was to be part of Cambridge University and devoted to science and technology. It was suggested that the new college be named after Churchill. When Colville relayed this suggestion to Churchill, his reaction was not one of immediate gratification – to have a memorial in his own lifetime, and in a university when, despite his many honorary degrees and Chancellorship of Bristol University, he had never gone to university, must have seemed strange. But Colville persisted: 'What memorial could be more lasting than a great university college?'

After a pause, WSC replied: 'It is very nice of them. And I ought certainly to be pleased. After all, it will put me alongside the Trinity.'

Anxious as he was to promote science and technology, Churchill saw that science for science's sake could be dangerous: 'Scientists should be on tap but not on top.' And, in the context of war, 'The latest refinements of science are linked with the cruelties of the Stone Age,' he commented in a speech in

March 1942. He also remarked, 'I have always considered that the substitution of the internal combustion engine for the horse marked a very gloomy milestone for the progress of mankind.'

But he also said: 'There ought to be a hagiology of medical science and we ought to have saints' days to commemorate the great discoveries which have been made for all mankind . . . a holiday, a day of jubilation when we can fête St Anaesthesia, and pure and chaste St Antiseptic . . . and if I had a vote I should be bound to celebrate St Penicillin.' (Penicillin had been used to treat Churchill when he had pneumonia in 1943. Though, according to Lord Moran's diaries, a staphylococcus infection that he contracted in June 1946 was stubbornly resistant to penicillin – whereupon Churchill remarked, 'The bug seems to have caught my truculence. This is its finest hour.')

✷

'When you have to kill a man it costs nothing to be polite,' Churchill wrote, referring to the ceremonial form of the declaration of war against Japan, 8 December 1941. It had been felt that Japan's behaviour – the almost simultaneous assaults on the US Pacific Fleet's base at Pearl Harbor and upon British and Dutch possessions in the Far East, including Malaya and Hong Kong, called for a more aggressive response.

Churchill was a great champion of liberty in all its forms (within reason, naturally), and he also recognized that liberty could mean liberty to be foolish, in speech especially: 'Where there is a great deal of free speech, there is always a certain amount of foolish speech.' And in a speech to the House of Commons in October 1943, he elaborated on this theme. 'Everyone,' he said, 'is in favour of free speech. Hardly a day passes without its being extolled, but some people's idea of it is that they are free to say what they like, but if anyone says anything back, that is an outrage.'

❈

'Mr Gladstone read Homer for fun, which I thought served him right.'

❈

Asked if he had bought a copy of the latest best-selling novel (said to be *Gone With the Wind*, published in 1937), Churchill answered sententiously 'There is a rule that before getting a new book, one should read an old classic.' He then hastened to add: 'Yet, as an author, I should not recommend too strict an adherence to this rule.'

'No, I only read for pleasure or for profit,' Churchill is supposed to have answered when asked by Lord Londonderry if he had read his last book.

✳

In an article on world affairs published in April 1938, Churchill, increasingly concerned by Britain's lack of preparedness against the growing German menace, said, 'We have never been likely to get into trouble by having an extra thousand or two of up-to-date aeroplanes at our disposal . . . As the man whose mother-in-law had died in Brazil replied, when asked how the remains should be disposed of: "Embalm, cremate, and bury. Take no risks!"'

✳

On painting: 'I prefer landscapes. A tree doesn't complain that I haven't done it justice.' And: 'I cannot pretend to feel impartial about colours. I rejoice with the brilliant ones and am genuinely sorry for the poor browns.'

✳

'There are men in the world who derive as stern an exaltation from the proximity of disaster and ruin, as others from success.'

'This is one of those cases in which the imagination is baffled by the facts,' WSC commented in a speech to the House of Commons in May 1941, referring to Rudolf Hess's parachute descent into Scotland.

✳

'Of this I am quite sure, that if we open a quarrel between the past and the present, we shall find we have lost the future.'

✳

'I am sure that the mistakes of that time will not be repeated; we should probably make another set of mistakes.' June 1944: Churchill was responding in the House to a call not to repeat the mistakes made after the First World War.

✳

At a time when Allied merchant and fishing vessels were under persistent attack from Germany, Churchill, in a BBC broadcast was able to offer some reassurance to the nation: 'I am glad to tell you . . . that the heat of their fury has far exceeded the accuracy of their aim.'

In 1941, in a minute to the Minister of Public Works and Buildings, who seemed to be allowing enthusiasm for his job to override the current circumstances, WSC felt constrained to urge him, 'Do not let plans for a new world divert your energies from saving what is left of the old.'

✳

Endorsing Pears Soap, WSC declared: 'Englishmen and Americans are divided by an ocean of salt water but united by a bathtub of fresh water and soap.' (His partiality for baths has elsewhere been commented on.)

✳

Asked why Lloyd George's Parliamentary Private Secretary, Sir Philip Sassoon, had been so lucky in his jobs, Churchill replied laconically, 'When you are leaving for an unknown destination, it is a good plan to attach a restaurant car at the tail of the train.'

✳

His valet, Norman McGowan, recalled how, when WSC was wearing the uniform of Lord Warden of the Cinque Ports during a tour of duty, one of his epaulettes fell off. He continued without it, but later that day remarked to McGowan, 'It's a good job I personally fasten my braces.'

During the last years of his life Churchill gradually withdrew from public life, spending his time quietly – sometimes in France, sometimes at Chartwell – where he would enjoy visits from friends, with whom he often played cards, or talked at length. At times he lamented that he was no longer capable of original thought – but would sometimes surprise himself by coming out with some sharp and shrewd comment. Even at the very end of his life, when it sometimes appeared that he was lost in a world of his own he would join in the conversation with a sudden and relevant remark.

'I know what it's like to be a log: reluctant to be consumed but yielding in the end to persuasion.' Churchill spoke these words as he gazed into a log fire, not long before his death.

✳

'Luckily, life is not so easy as all that; otherwise we should get to the end too quickly,' Churchill wrote in *My Early Life* (1930). He ensured he had more than enough to fill his ninety years of life not to get to the end too quickly.